Doodle
Numbers
Taro Gomi

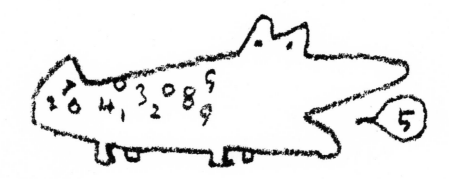

 **Thames & Hudson**

Draw **1** piece of cake.

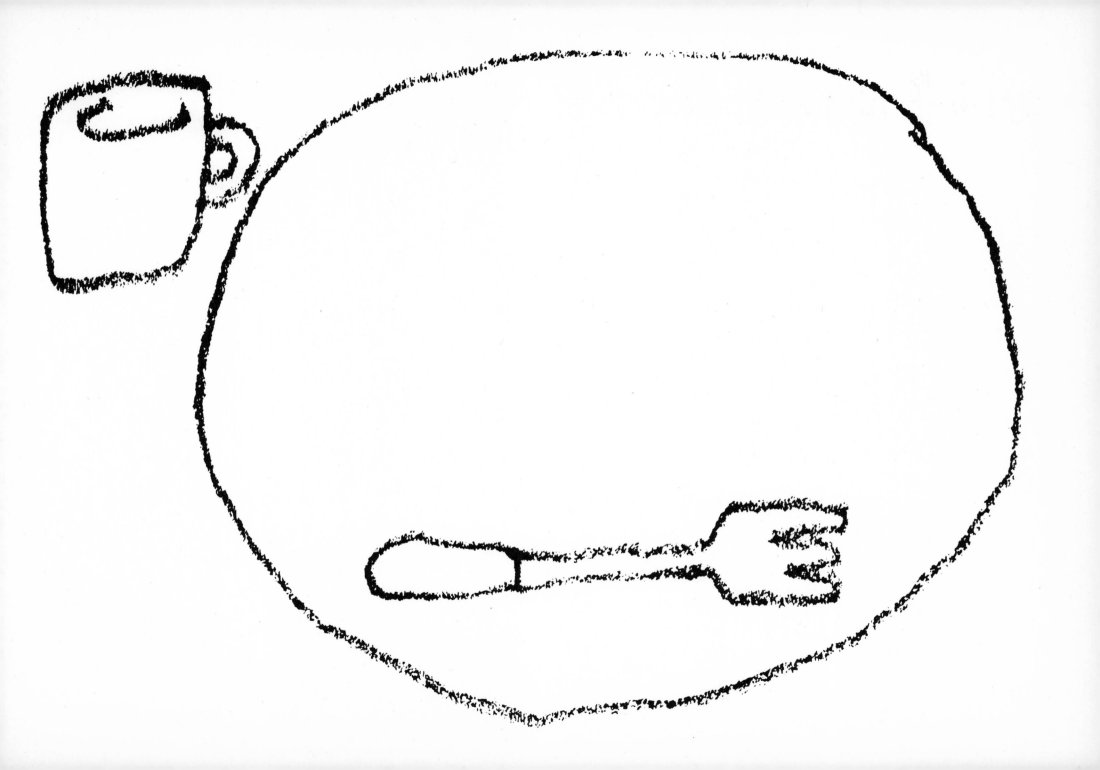

Draw **2** puppies.

Draw **3** chickens.

Draw **4** plates on the table.

Draw **5** pencils.

Draw **5** lines in the notebook too.

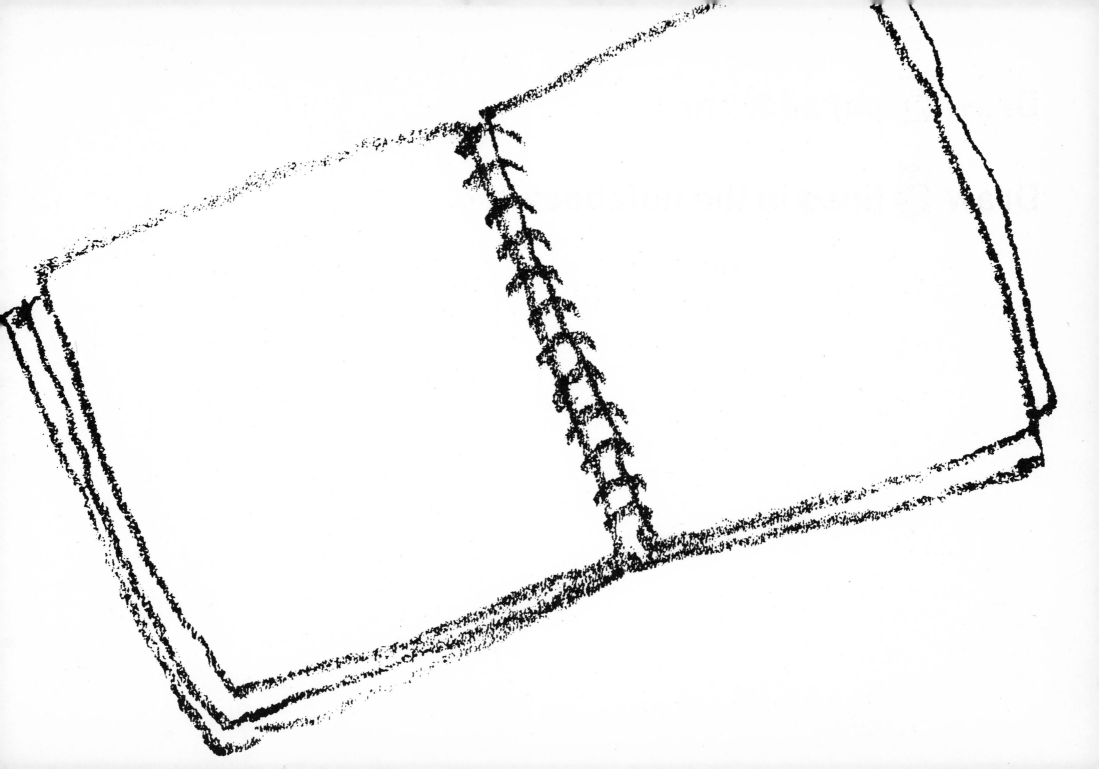

Draw **6** sheep in the field.

Draw **6** cows too.

Draw **7** planes flying in the sky.

Draw **8** boats sailing on the sea.

Then draw **8** fish swimming in the water.

Draw **9** children playing in the playground.

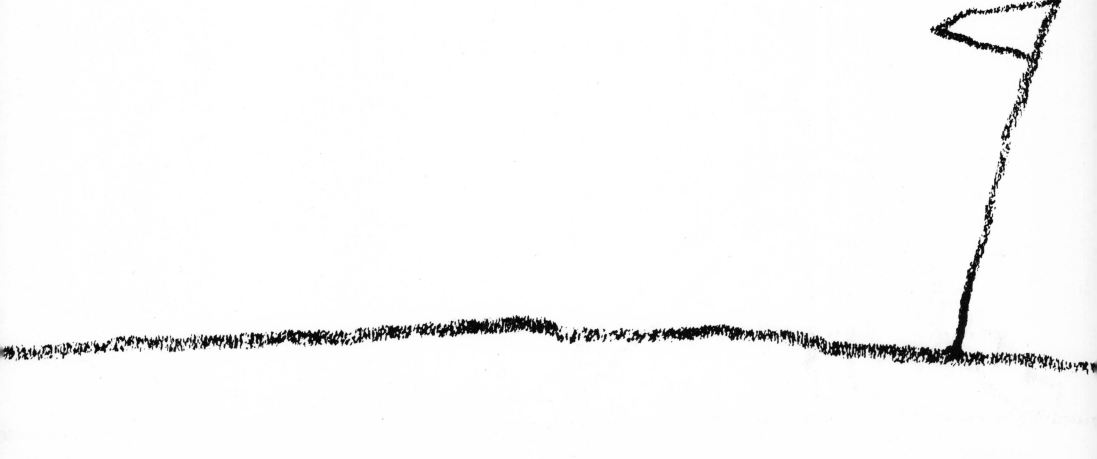

Draw **10** houses to make a street.

Draw **10** trees too.

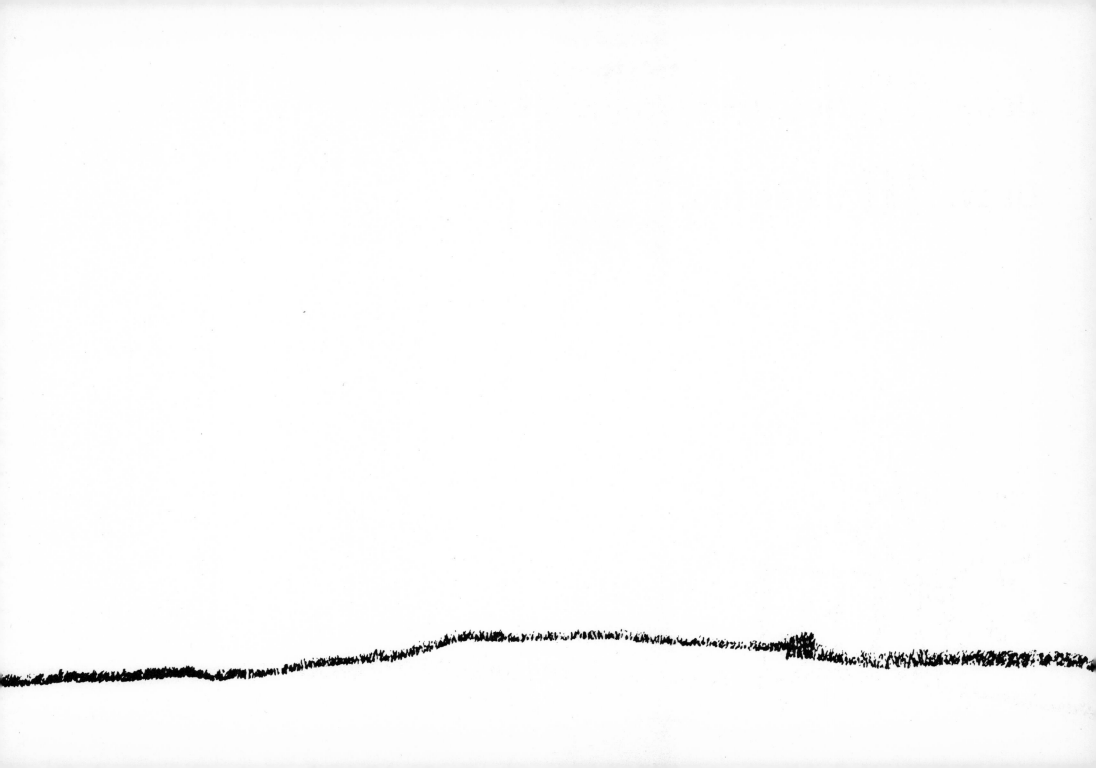

Write the number 1 on the flag.

Write the number 2 on the side of the truck.

Write the number 3 on the boy's shirt.

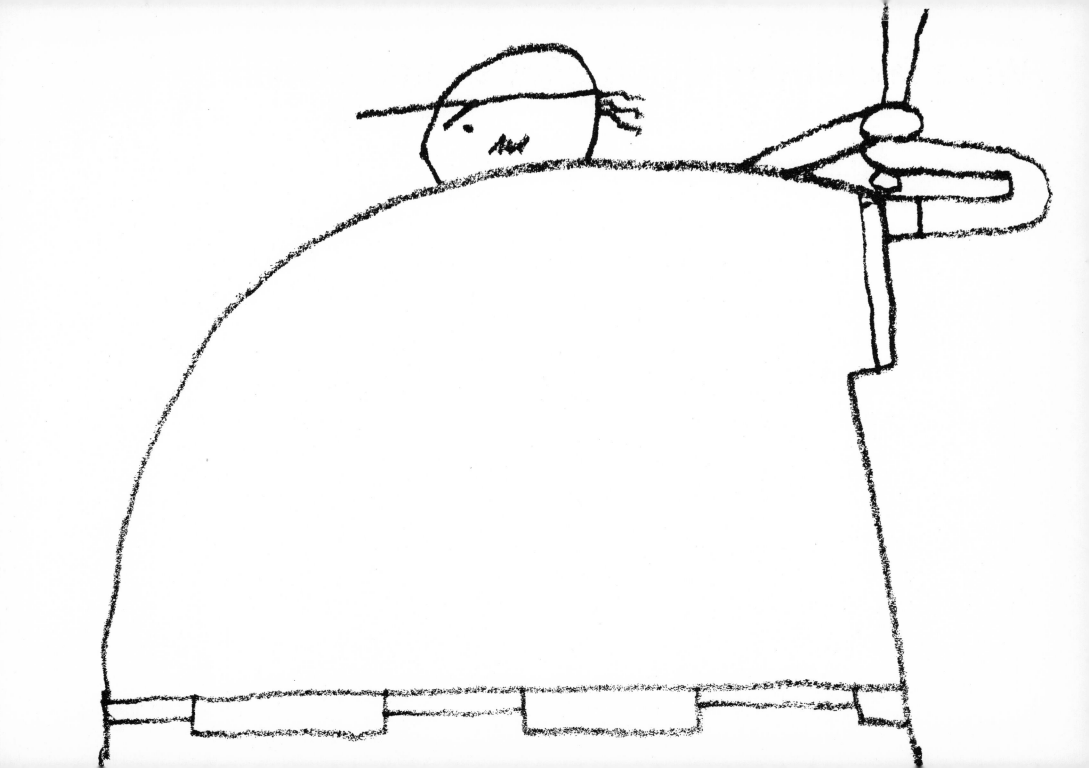

Circle the 4th day of the month on the calendar.

CALENDAR

		1	2	3	4	5
6	7	8	9	10	11	12
13	14	15	16	17	18	19
20	21	22	23	24	25	26
27	28	29	30	31		

Write the number 5 on the side
of this building with 5 floors.

Write the number 6 on the player's jersey.

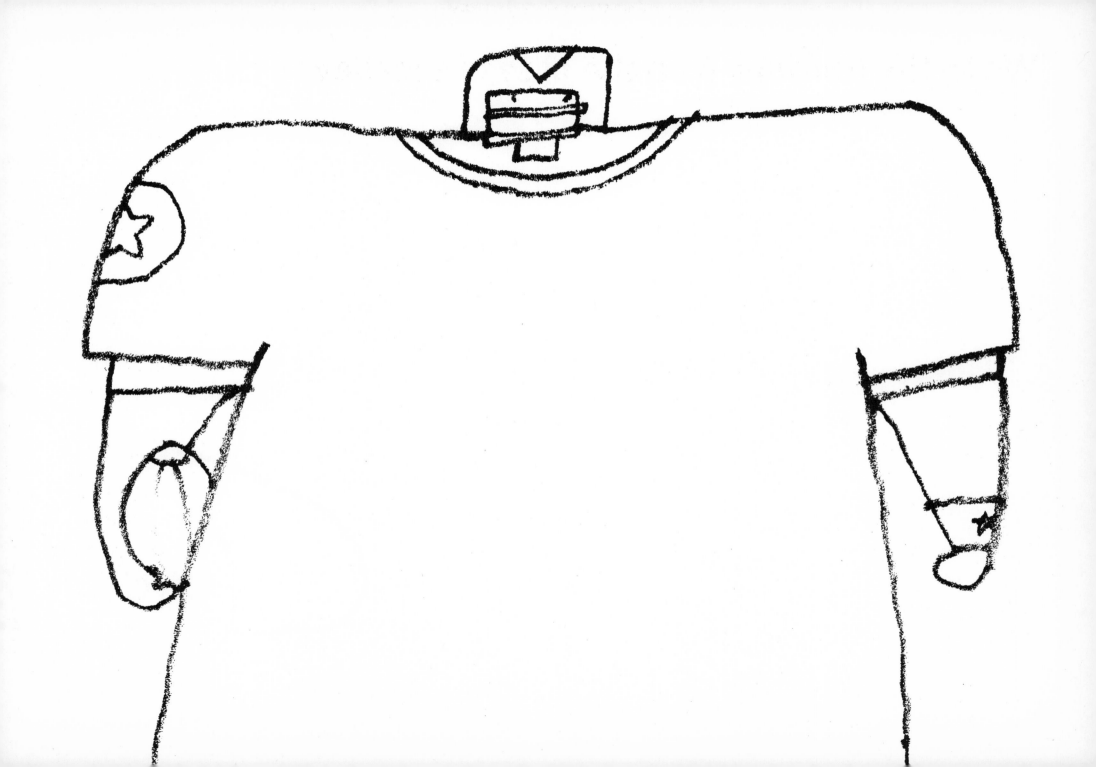

Write the number 7 on the side of the racing car.

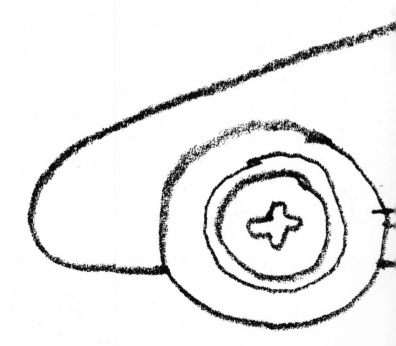

Write the number 8 on the train platform.

Write the number 9 on the clock.

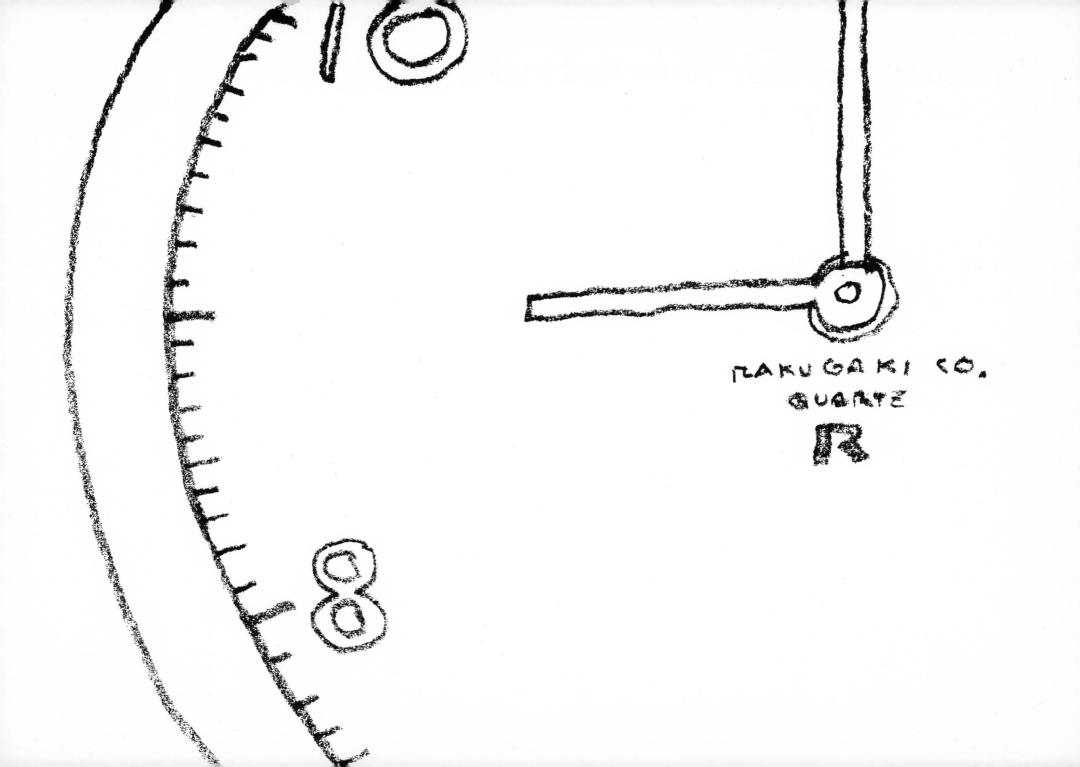

RAKUGAKI CO.
QUARTZ

Write the number 10 on the scoreboard.

Well done, you scored full marks!

Write 1, 2, 3 to help this boy to take a big jump!

Write your lucky number inside this star.

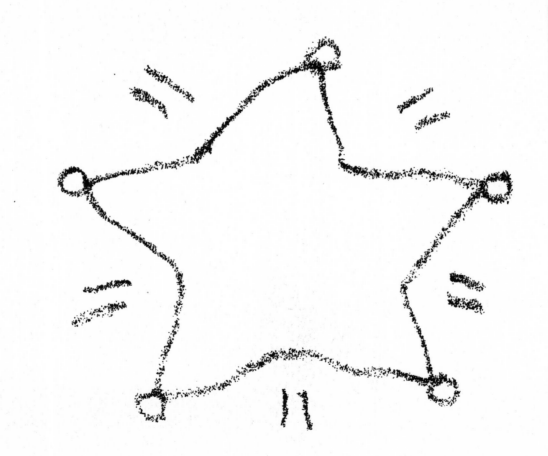

Write your unlucky number inside this star.

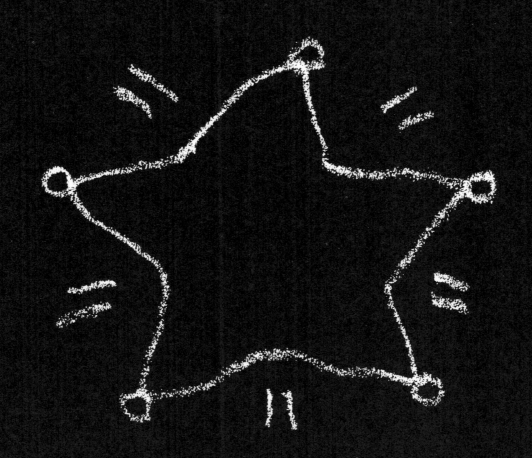

Draw lots of number 1s growing in this field.
The farmer will harvest them all.

Draw lots of number 6s growing in this tree.
The girl will pick them and put them in her basket.

Draw lots of number 8s flying like butterflies.

The boy will catch them in his net.

These numbers are written with string.
Find something you can use to write 1, 2, 3!

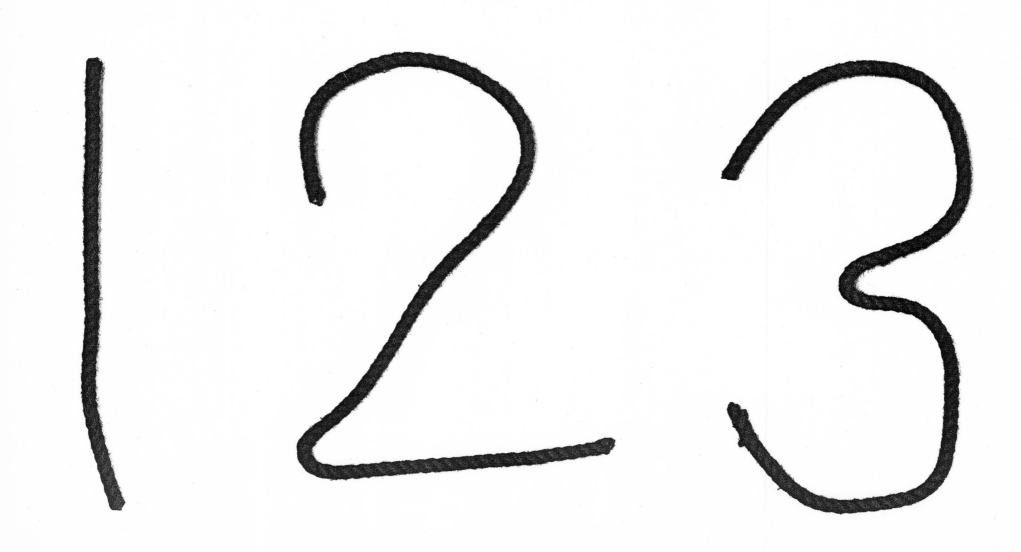

These numbers are written with wire.
Find something you can use to write 4, 5, 6!

These numbers are written with paper clips.
Find something you can use to write 7, 8, 9!

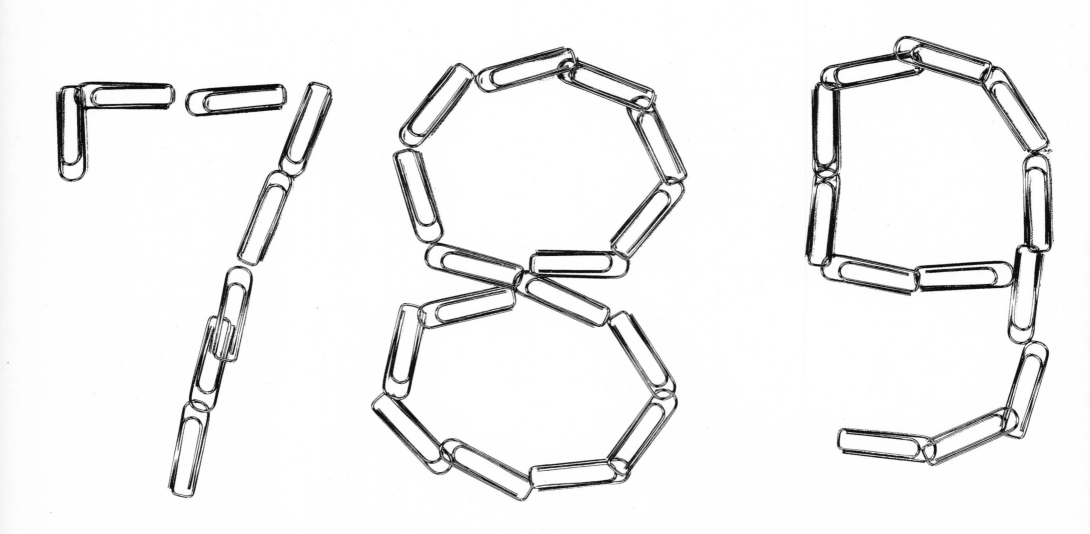

This number is made of plasticine.
Find something you can use to make a number 10!

These numbers are made from a shoelace.
Can you make numbers in the same way?

Only one house in this street has a number.
Write numbers on the other houses too.

Only one of these blocks has a number.
Write numbers on the other blocks too.

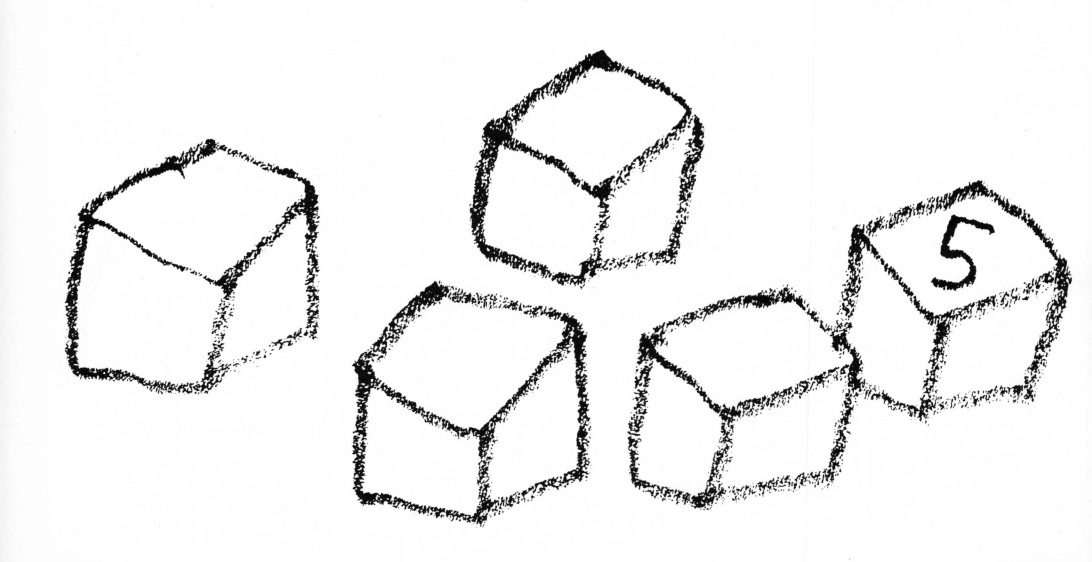

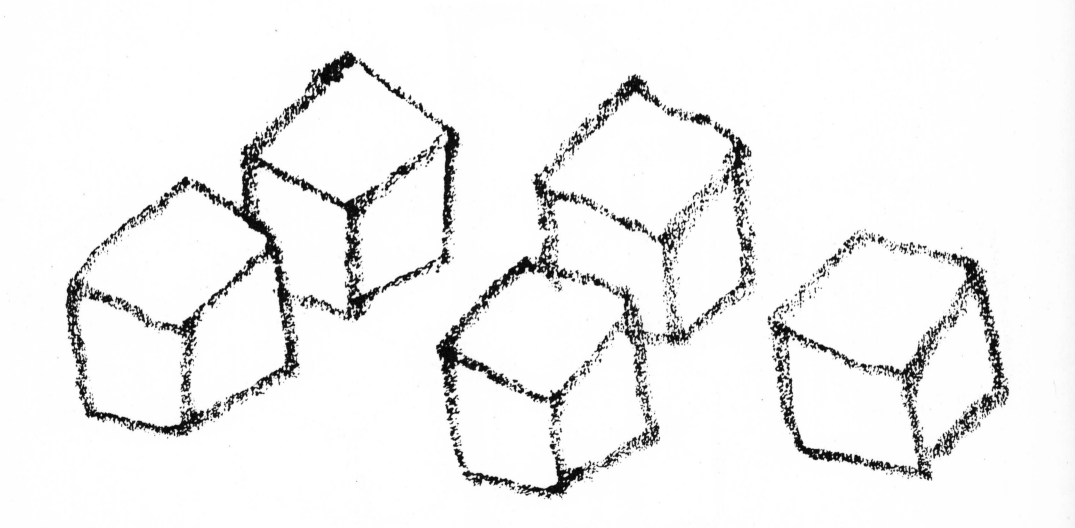

The number 1 has been turned into a penguin.

Turn the other numbers
into animals too.

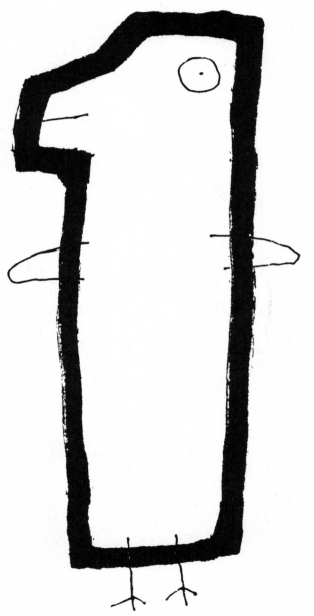

2

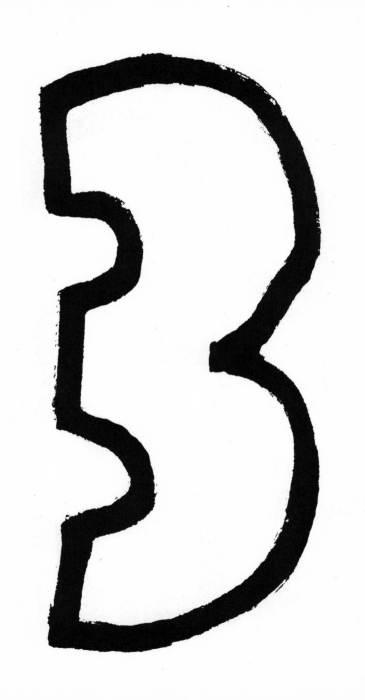

10

Only one locker in this row has a number.

Fill in the numbers on the other lockers.

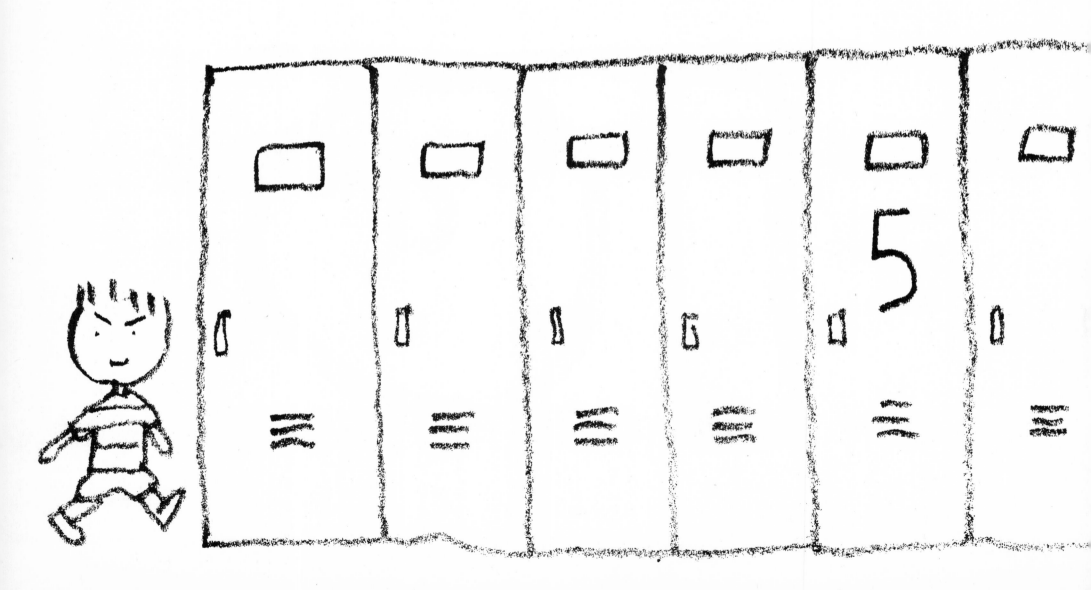

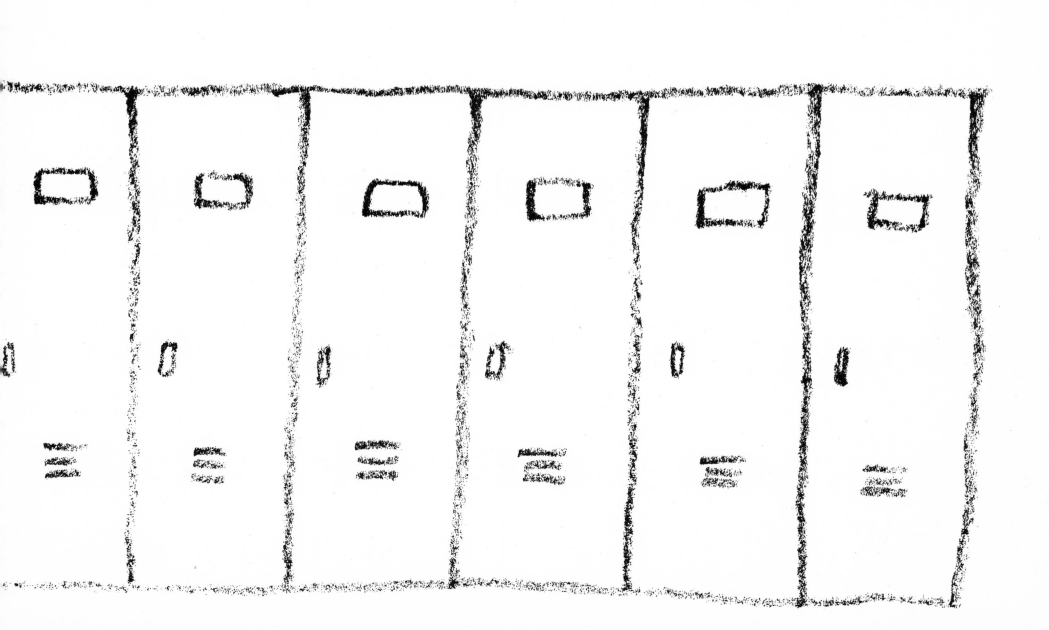

Fill in the numbers on these lockers too.

They begin with number 31.

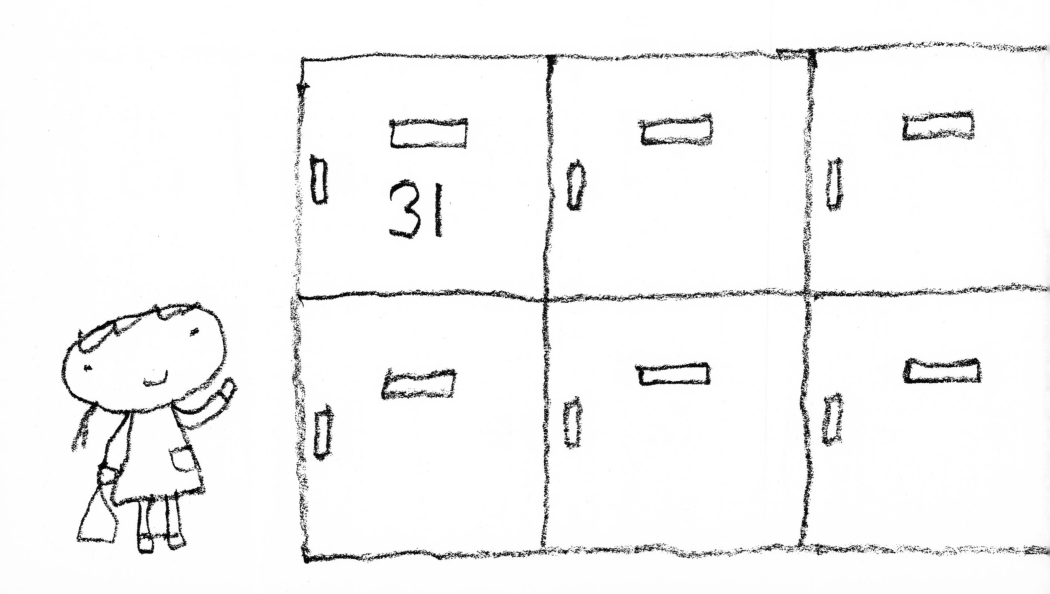

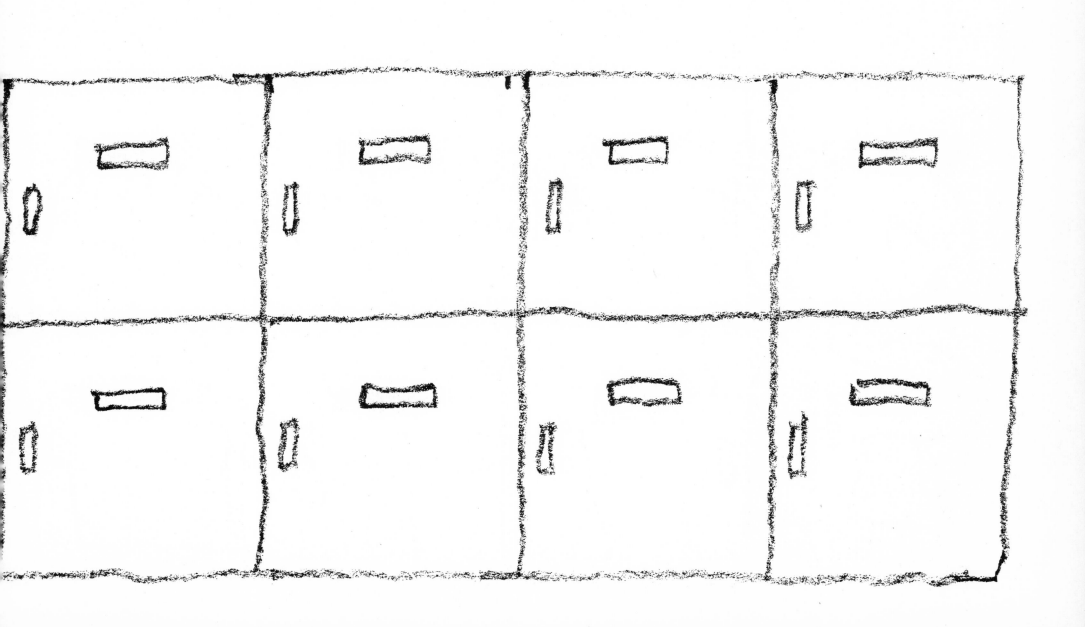

Write numbers on the children's t-shirts.

Write numbers on the backs of the team's shirts.

Write numbers on the balloons.

Write numbers on the flags.

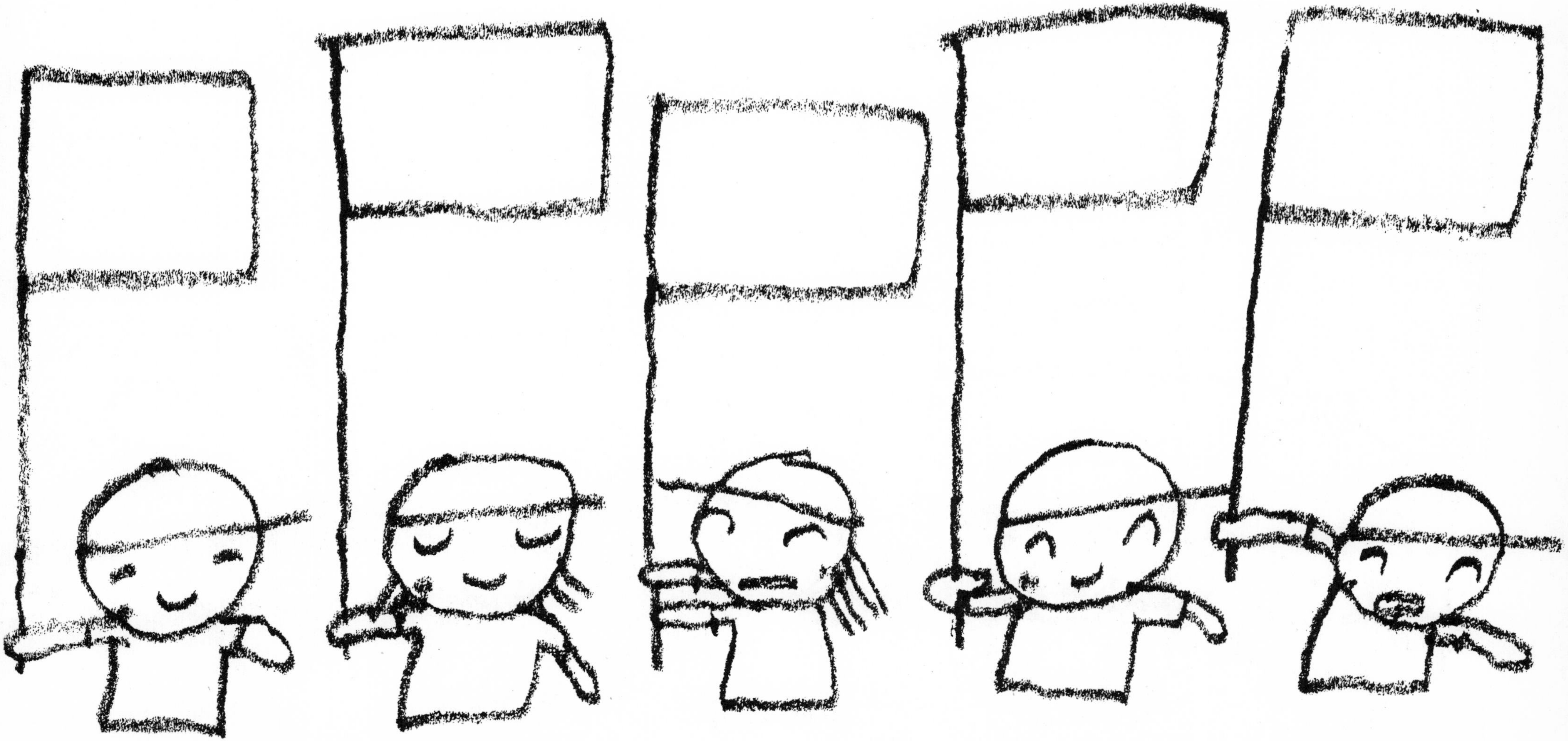

Write numbers on the train carriages.

It's a very long train!

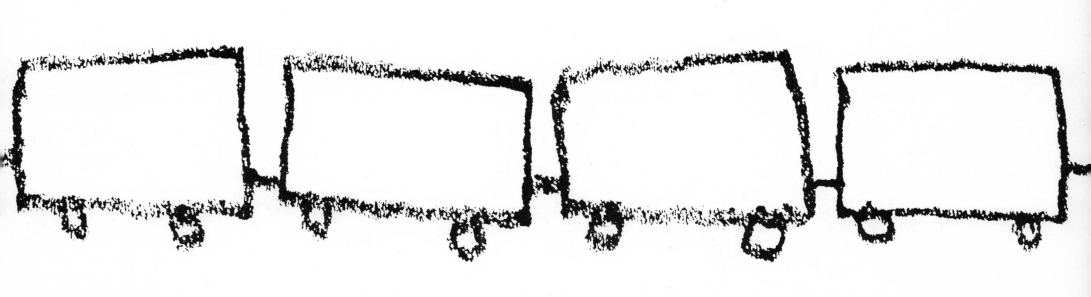

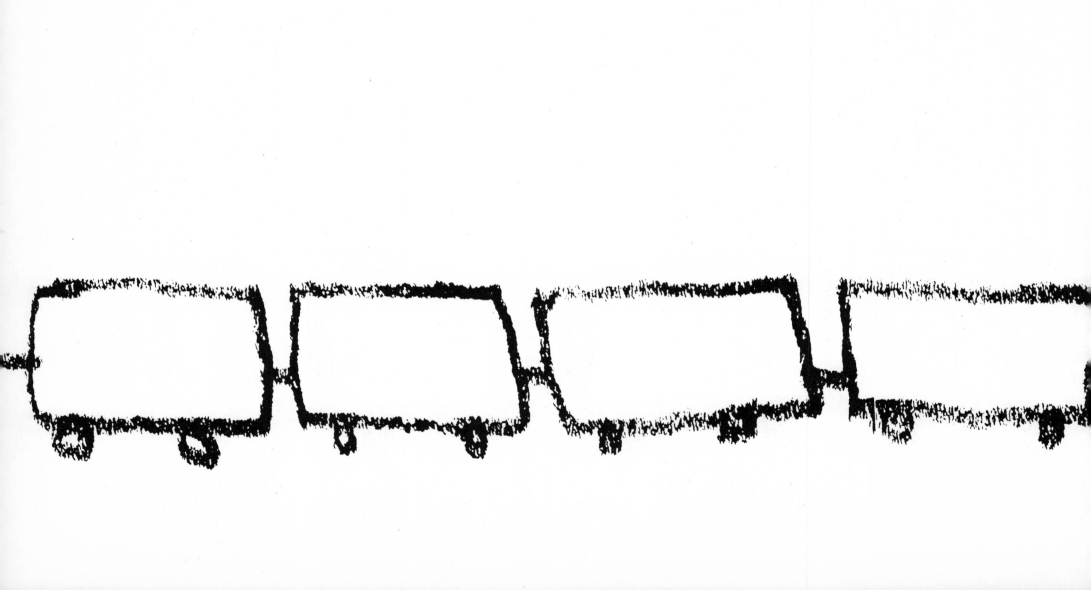

Now try writing numbers on this train,
beginning from the back.

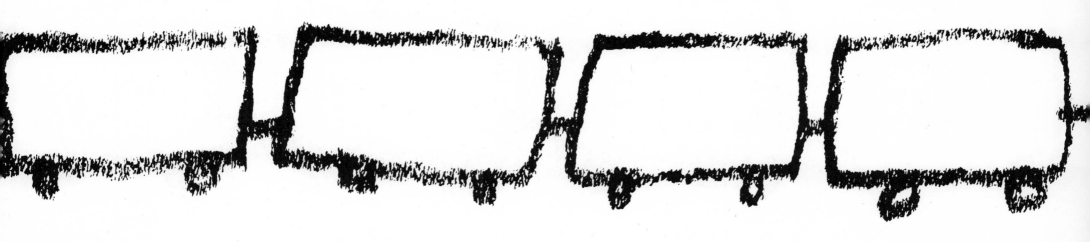

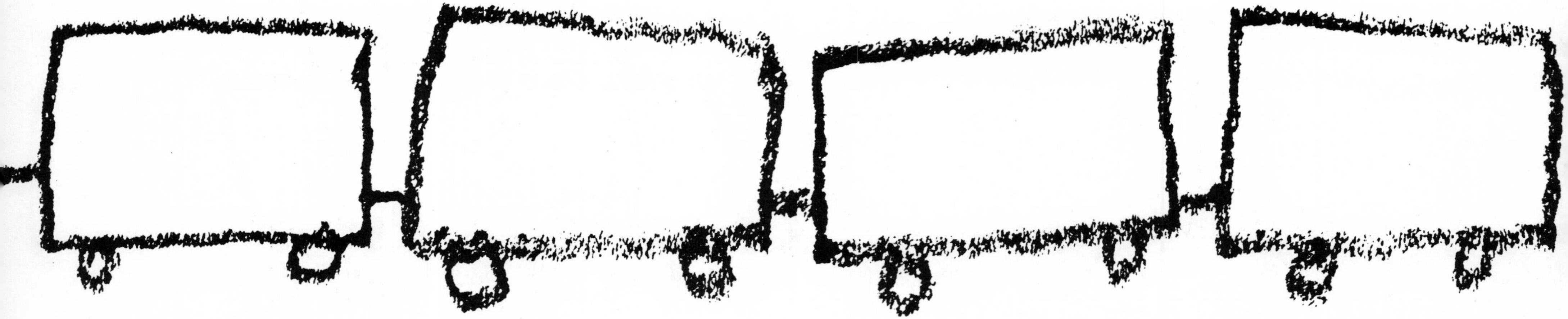

Write numbers on the snake's stripes.

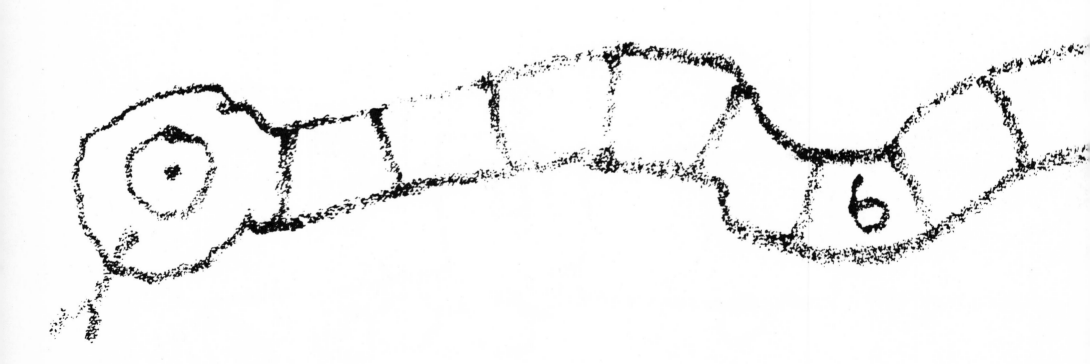

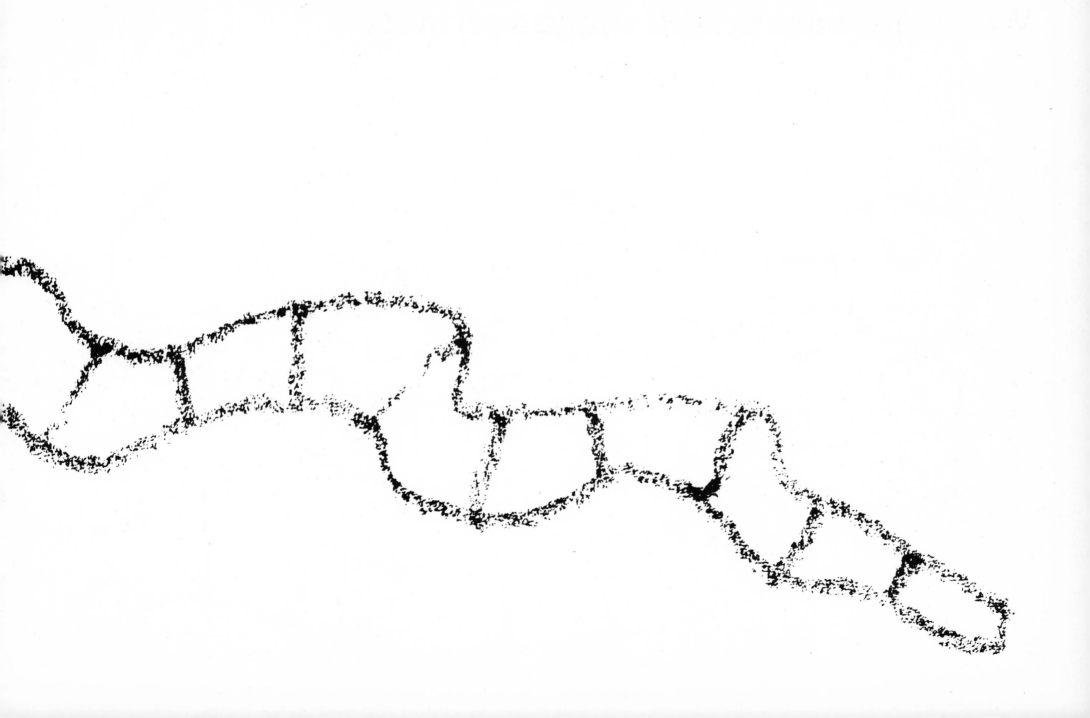

Now do the same with this longer snake.

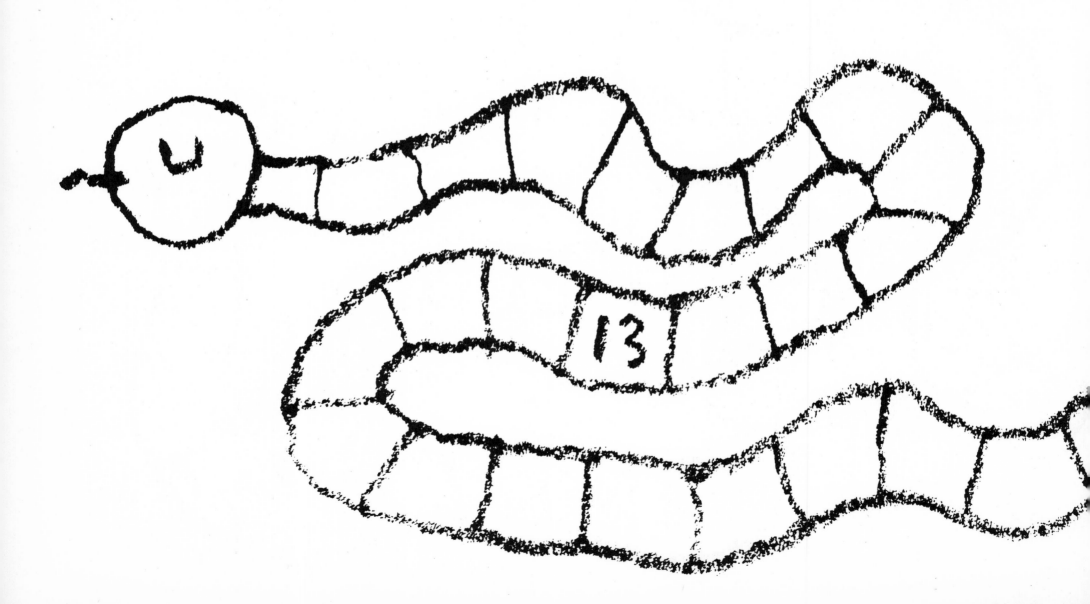

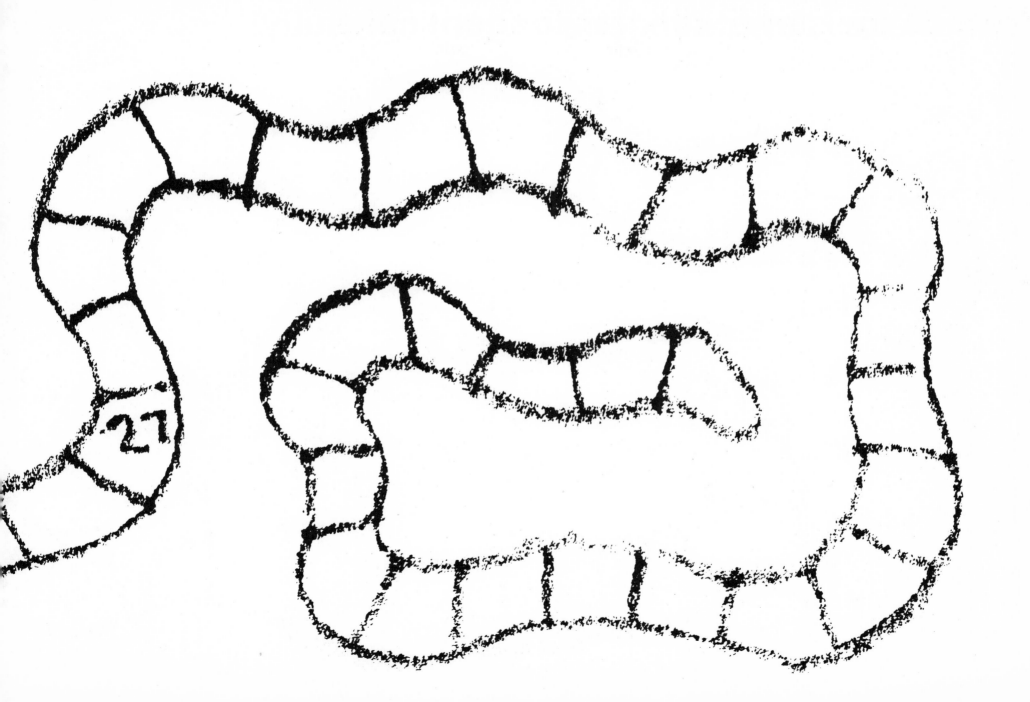

This snake is even longer, so count carefully!

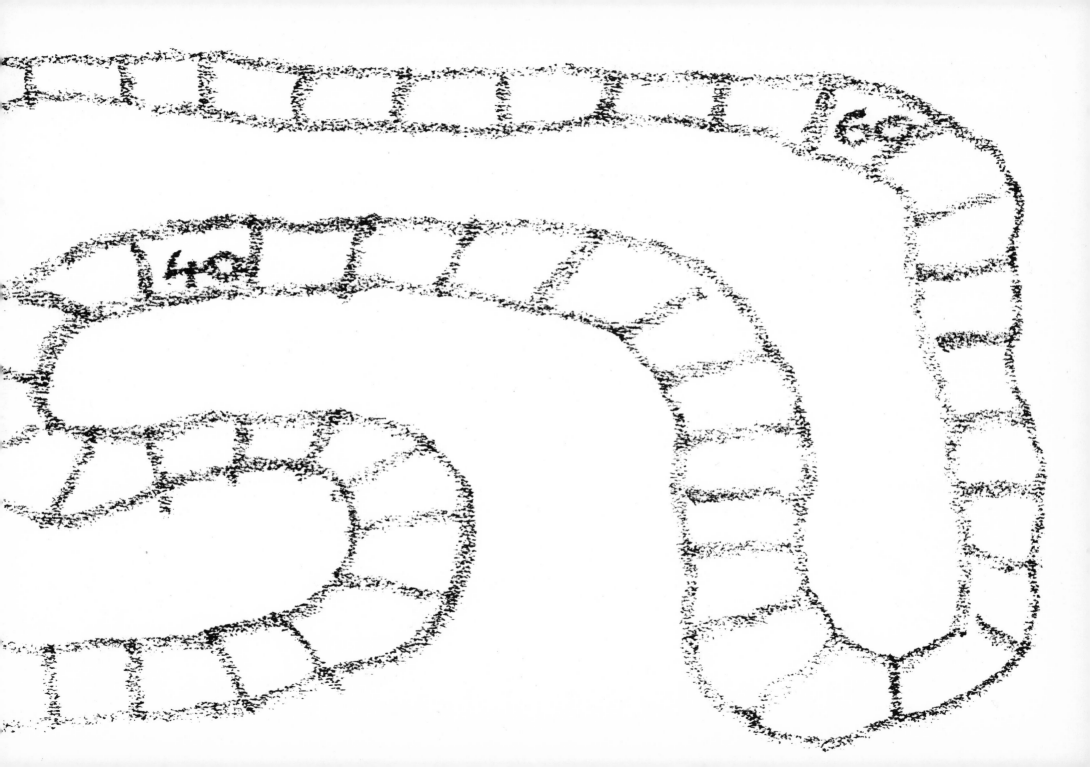

How many houses can you see?
Draw roads to link them together.

How many fish can you see?
When you've counted them all, colour them in.

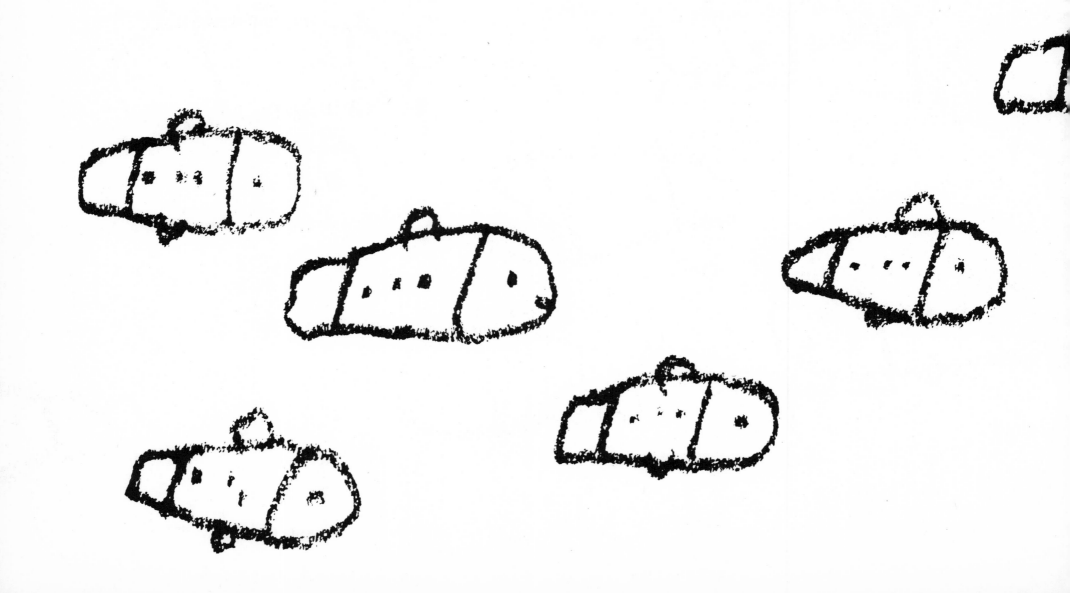

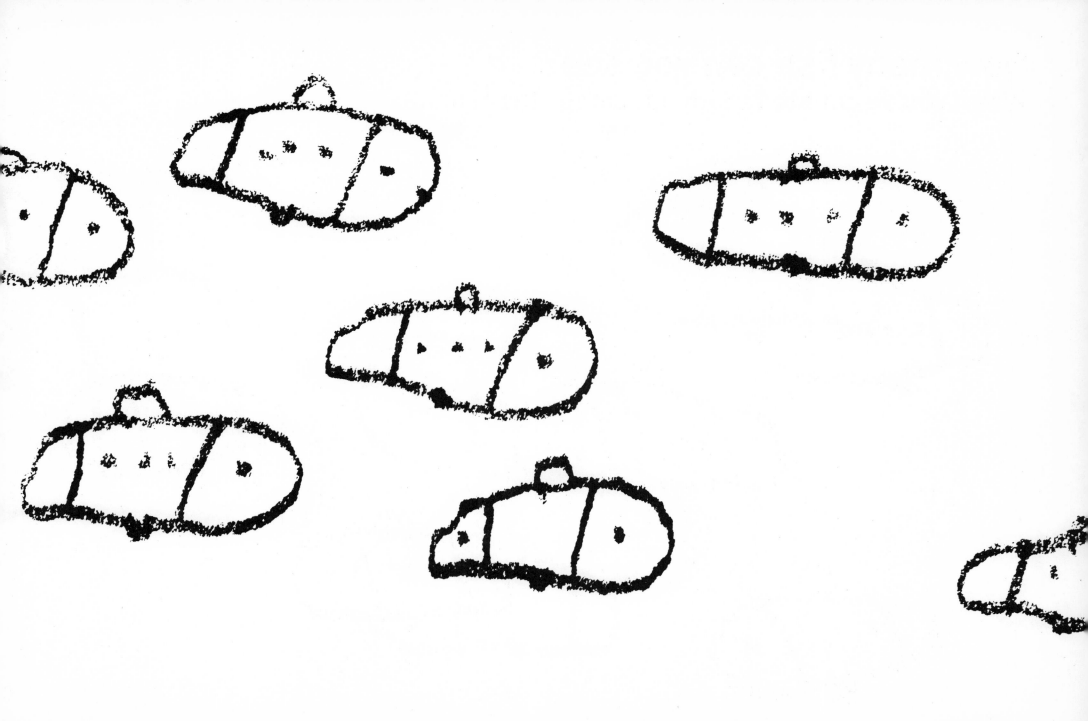

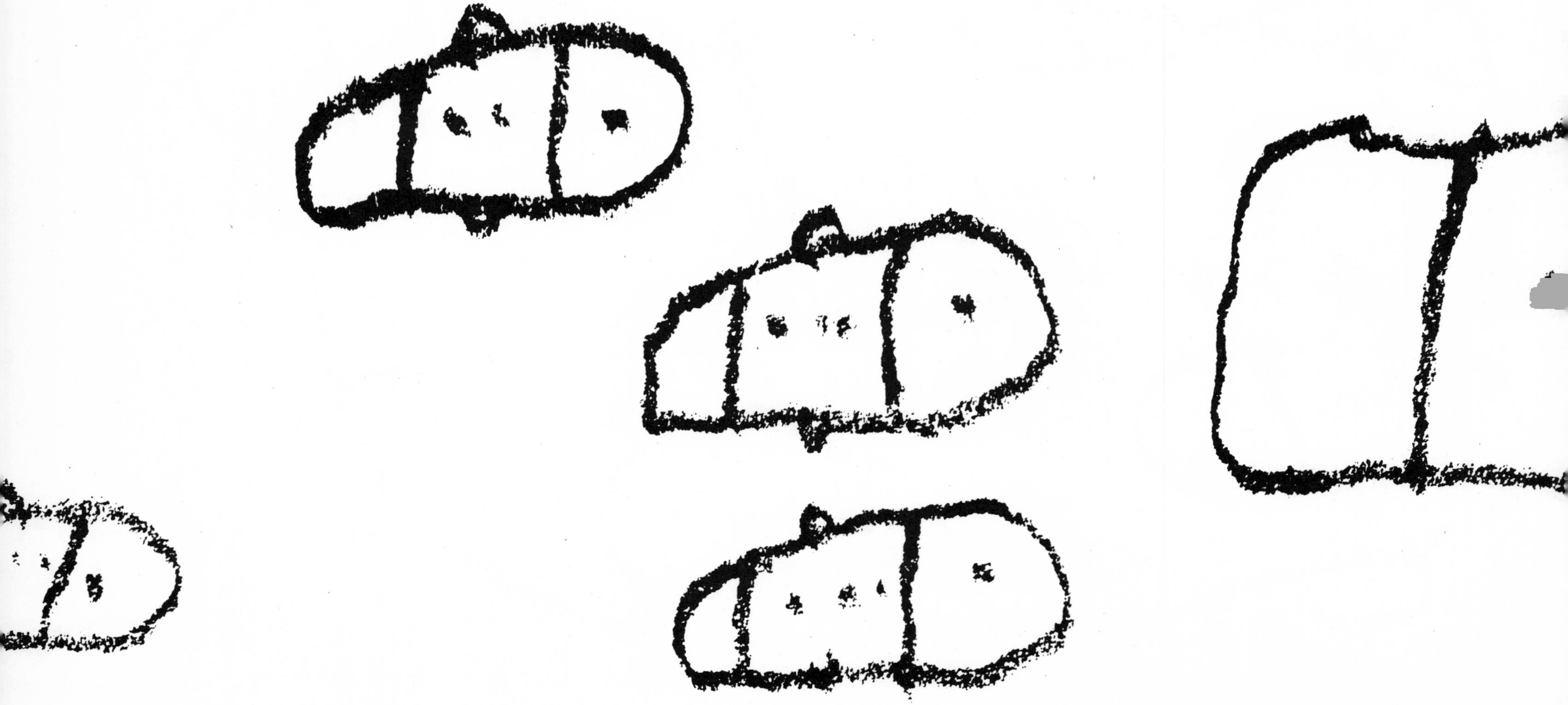

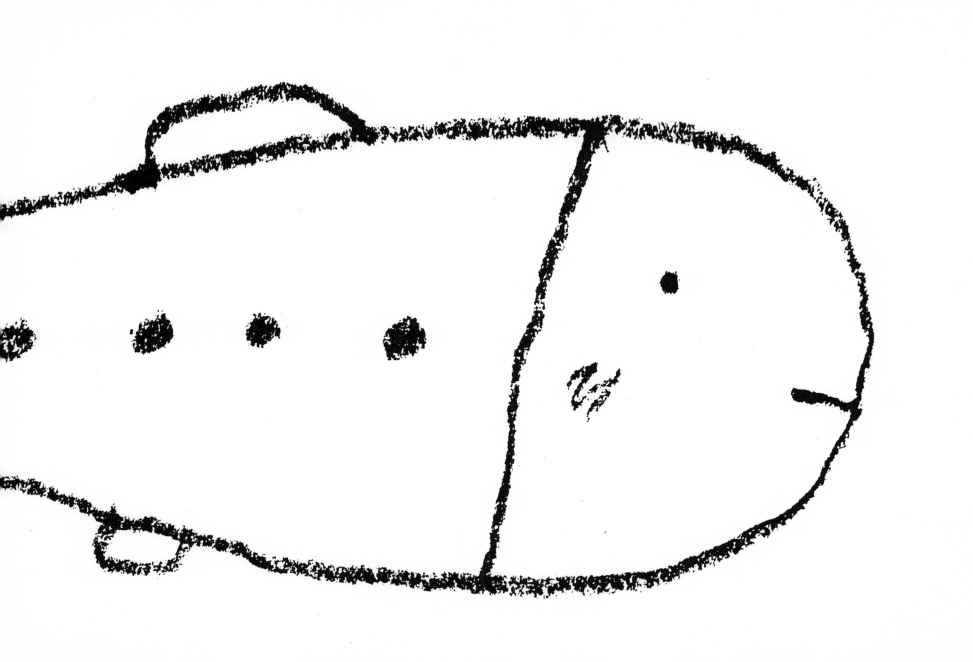

Colour this rainbow with 7 stripes.

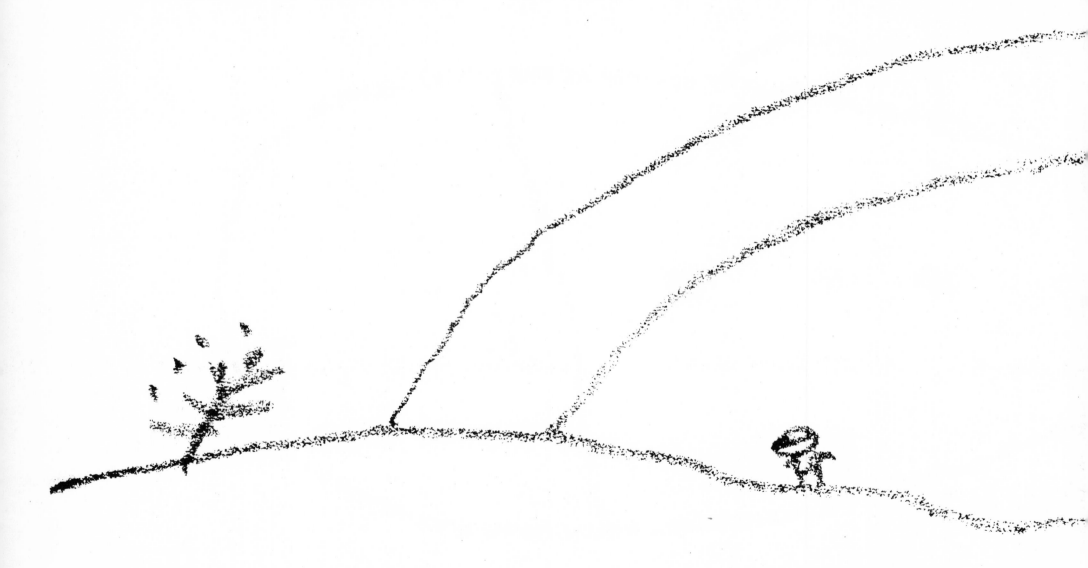

How many wheels can you see on this truck?
Draw the same number of boxes on the back of the truck.

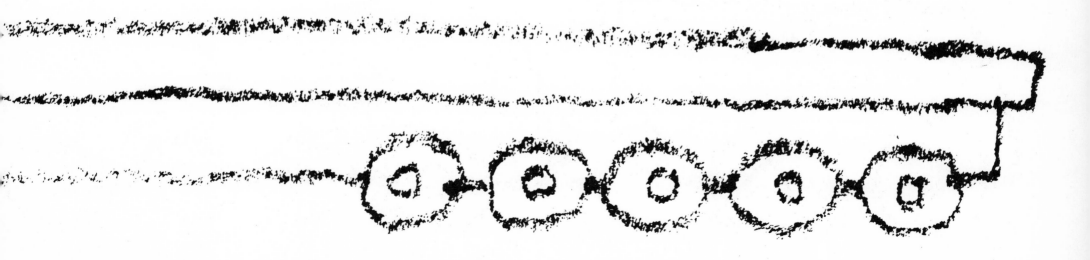

How many eyes does the cat have?
How many ears?
How many whiskers?

How many legs does the octopus have?

How many legs does the crab have?
And how many claws?

How many legs does the centipede have?

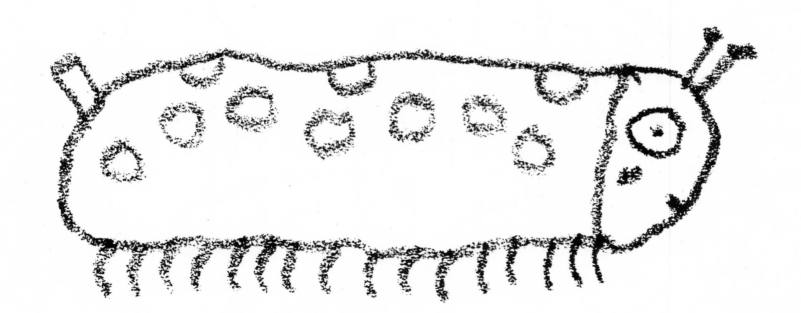

How many legs does the jellyfish have?

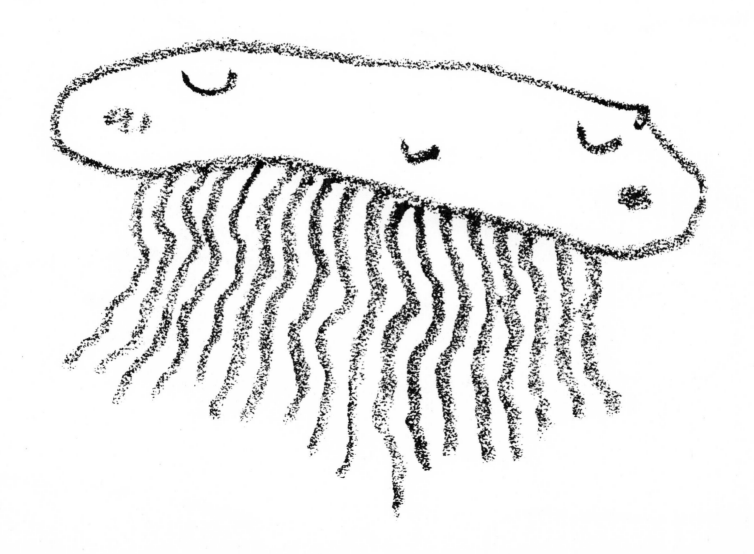

How many teeth does the crocodile have?

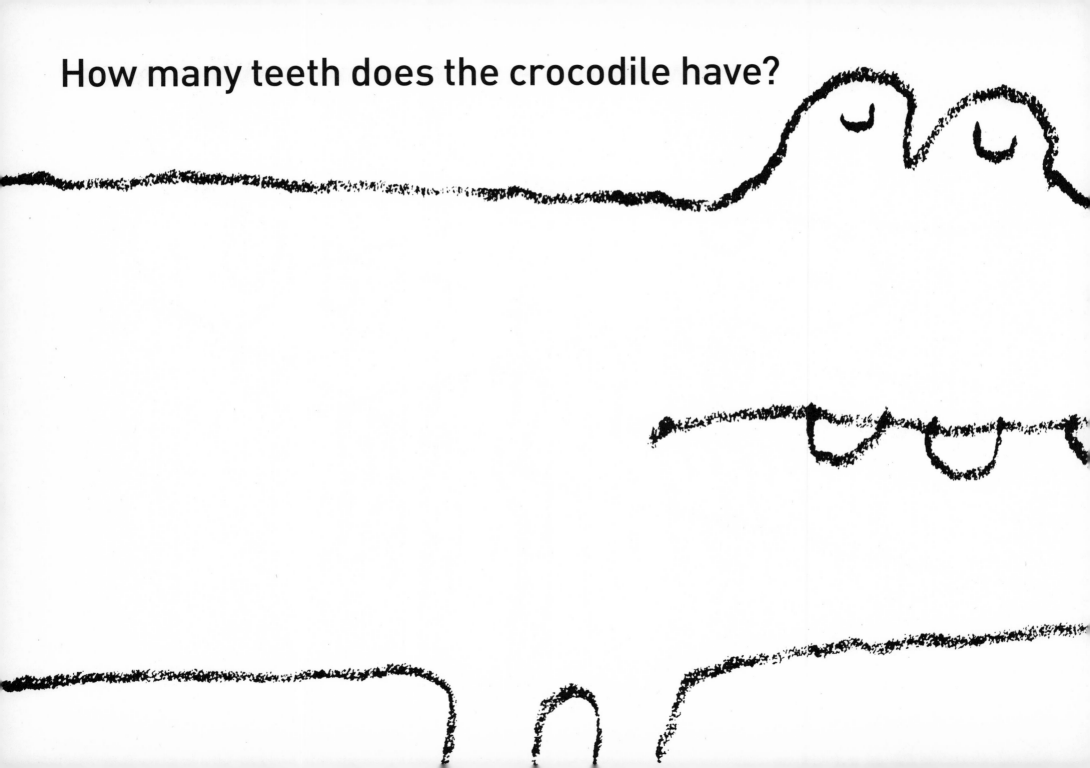

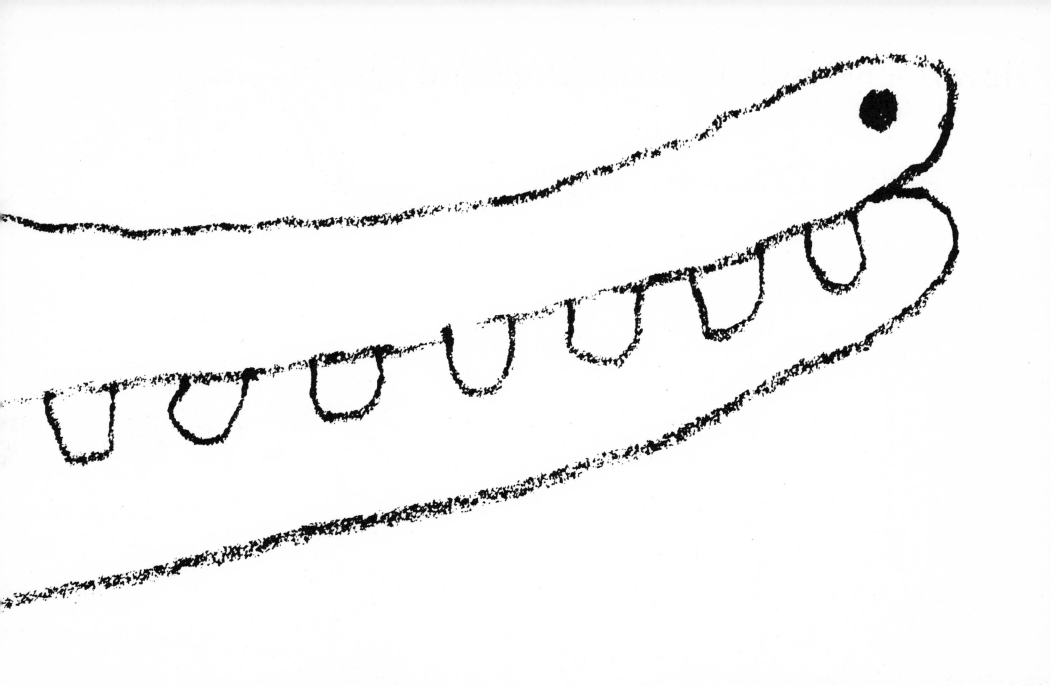

Surprise! There are more teeth!
Count them again.

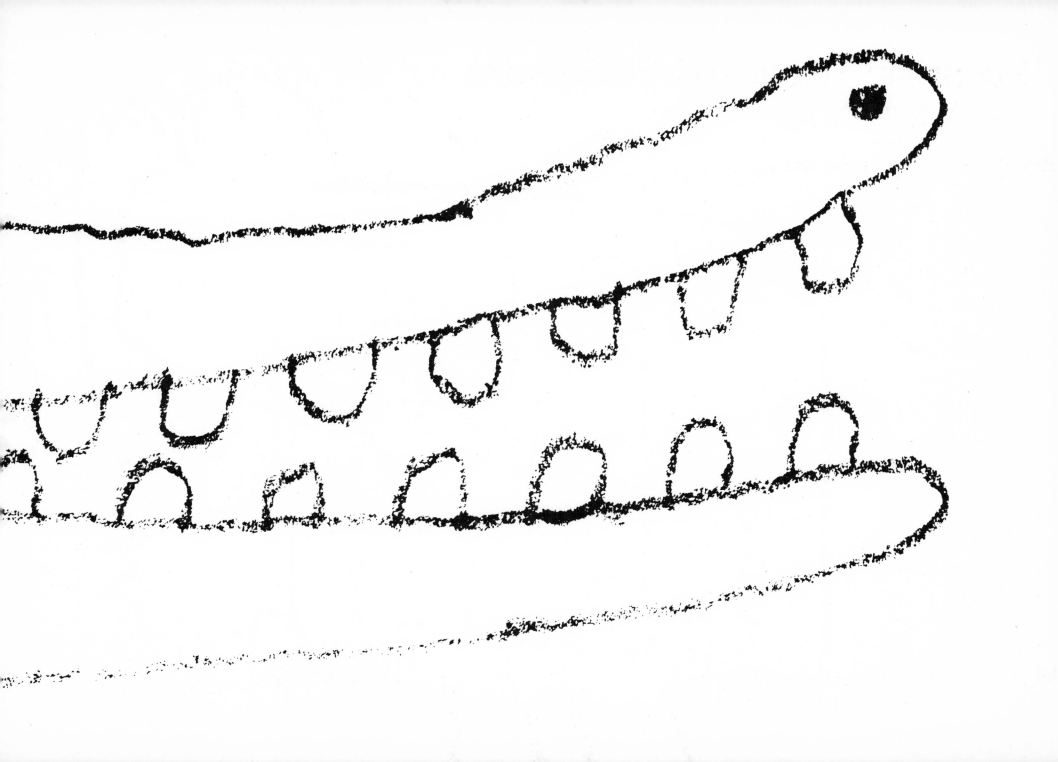

Write the numbers on the phone.
Add some symbols too.

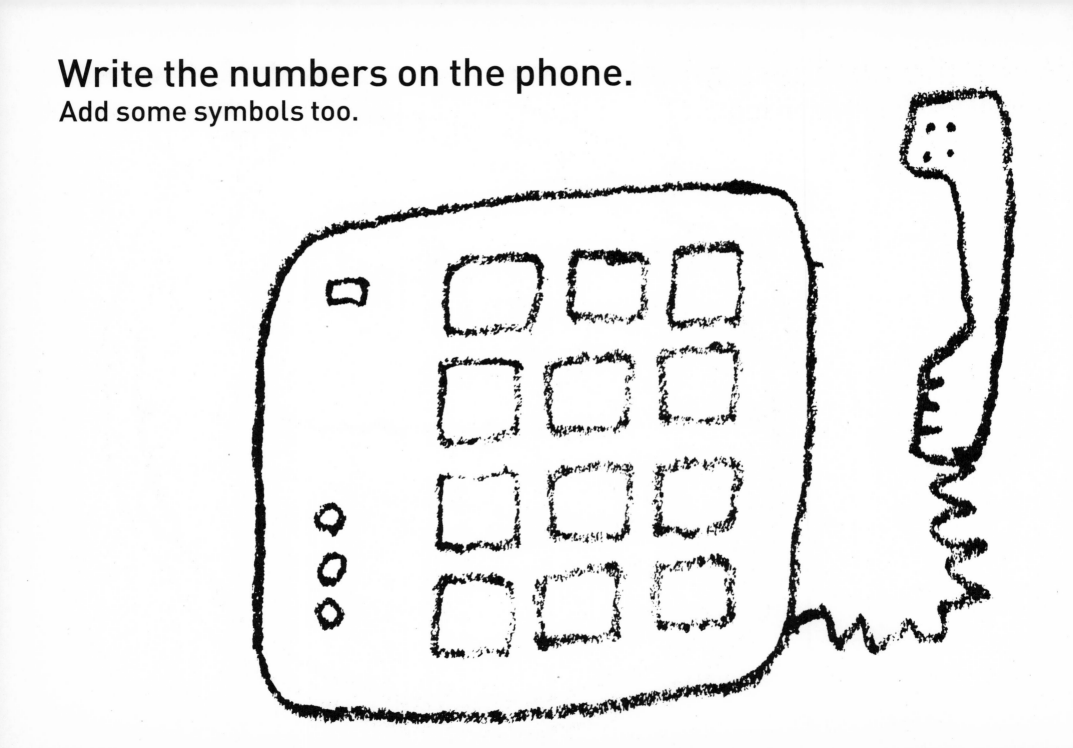

Write the numbers on this clock.
Draw the second hand too.

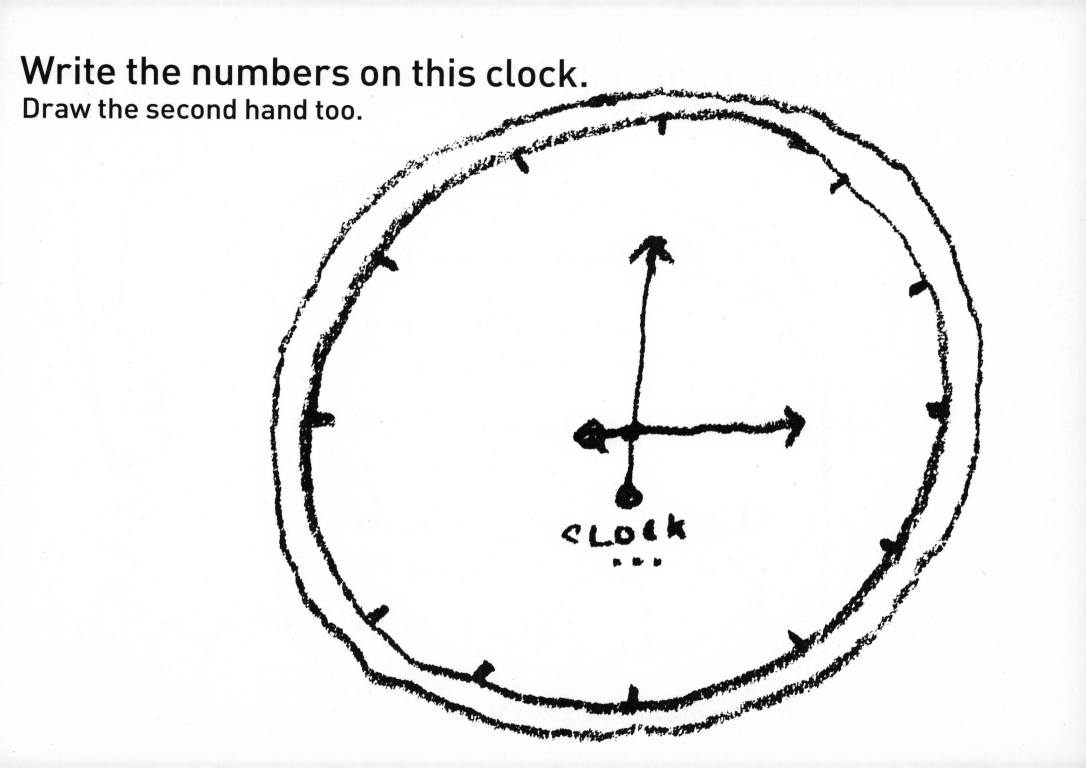

CLOCK

Draw the hands on the clock.

It's 7 o'clock.

Now it's 3:45 and 15 seconds!

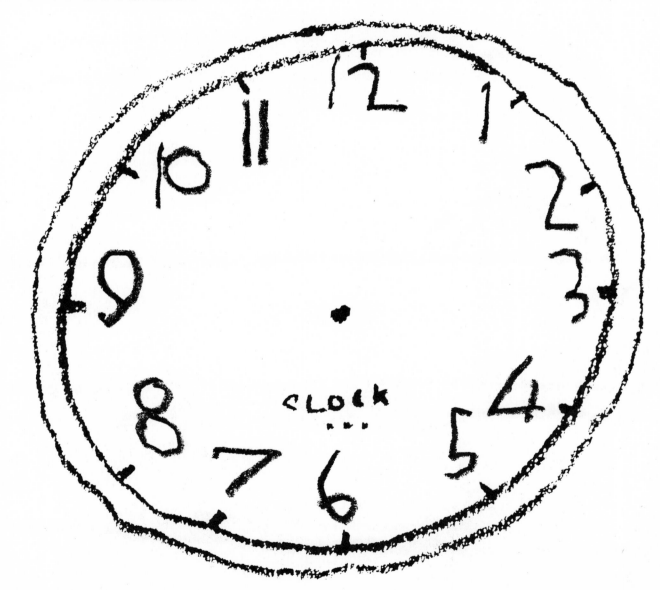

These cars have empty number plates.
Write some numbers and letters on them.

How many candles are there?
Write the number in the middle of the cake.

And how many candles on this cake?

Draw pictures on these stamps.
Don't forget to add the price of each one.

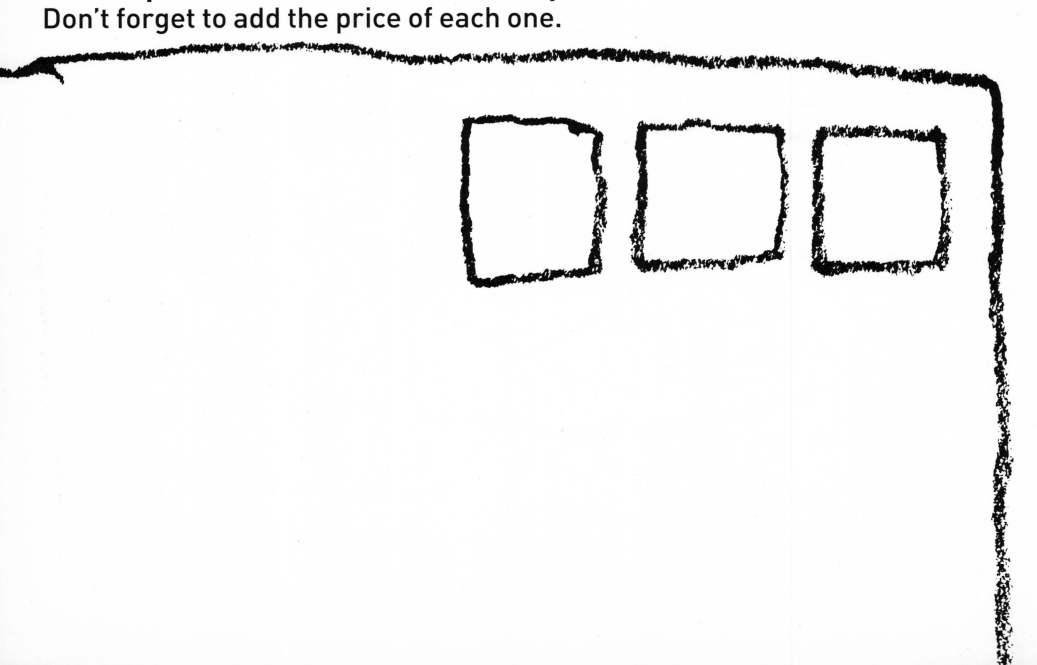

Write the address on this envelope.

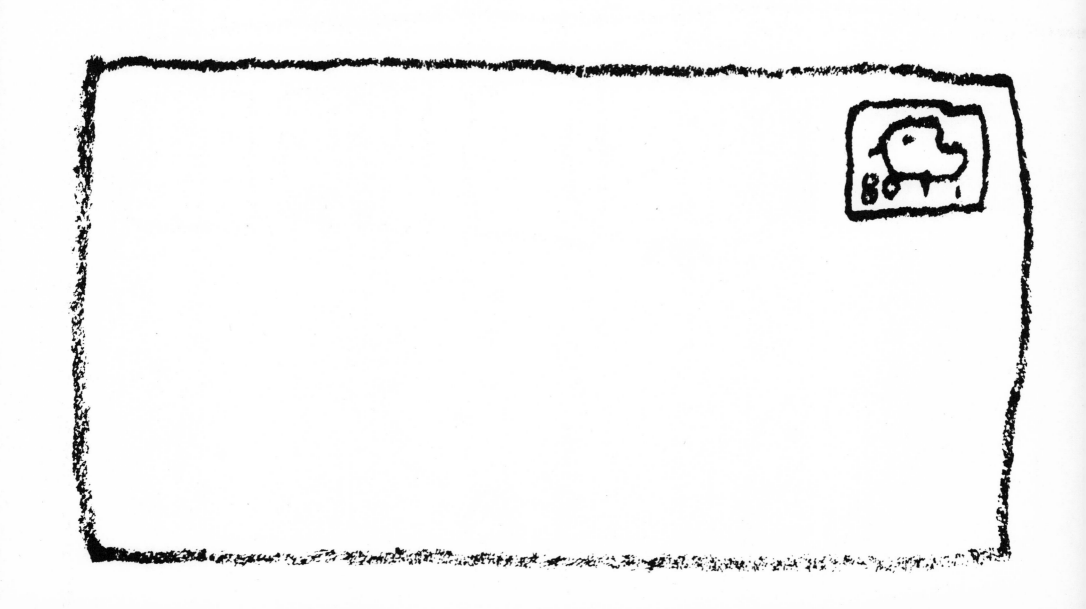

Colour 3 of the strawberries red.
The rest aren't ripe yet!

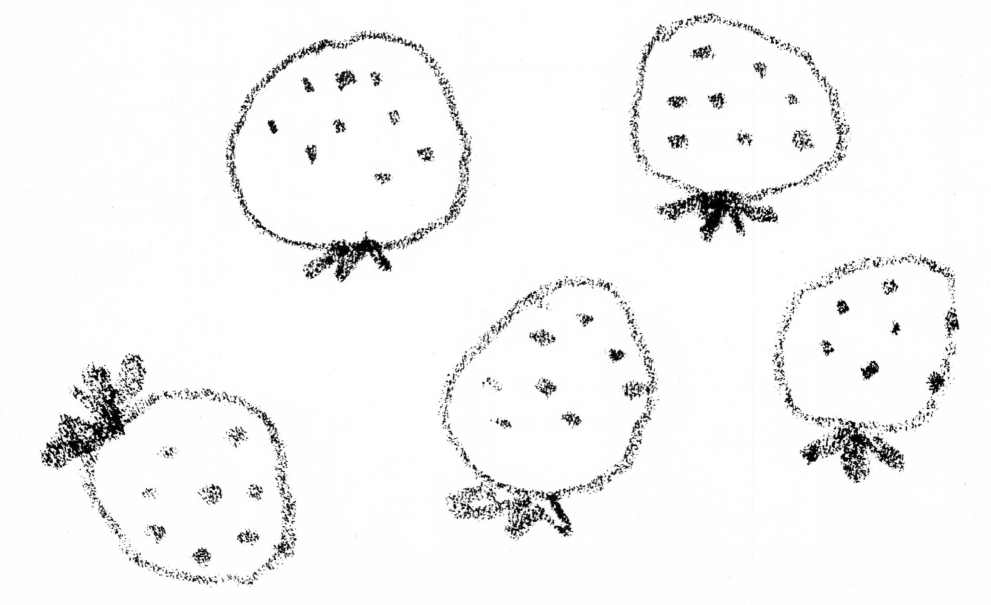

Colour 10 of the apples green.

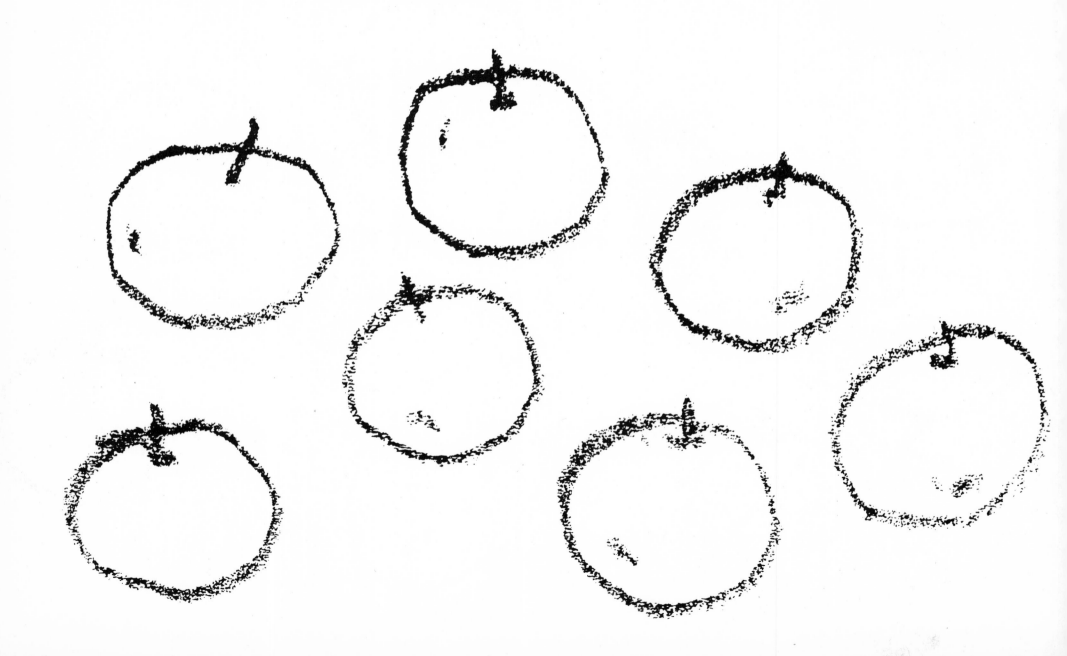

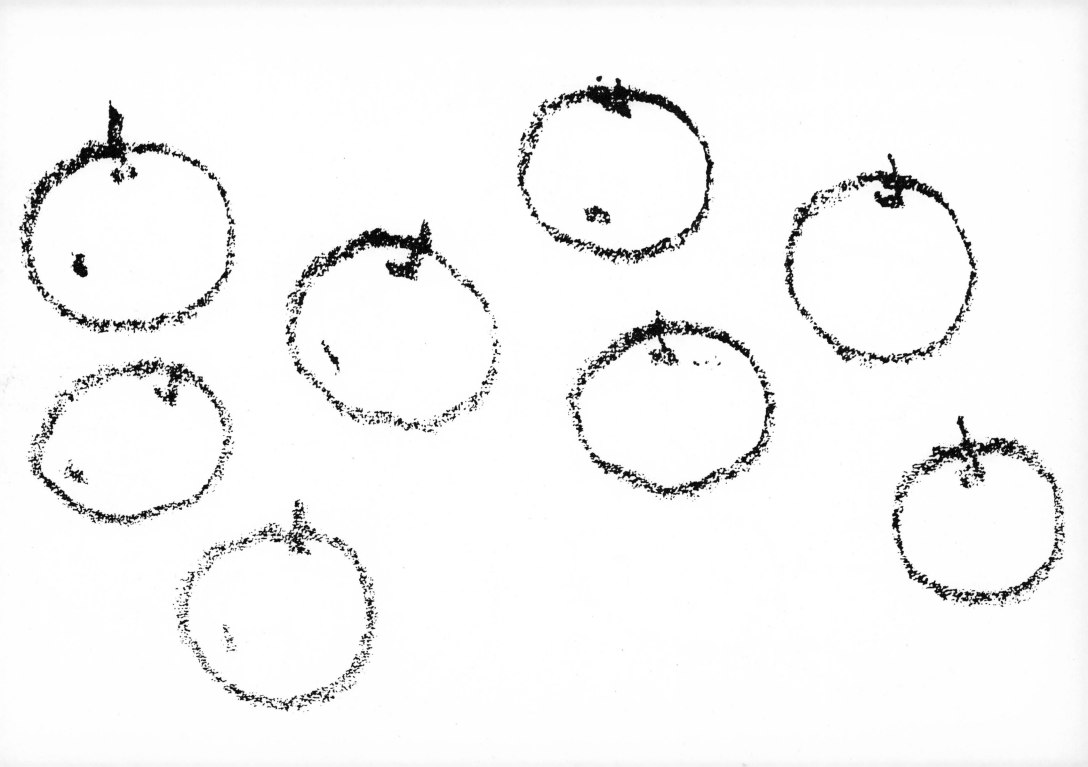

Three black cats, three ginger cats,
and three stripey cats.
Colour them in.

Colour 4 red flowers and 8 yellow flowers.

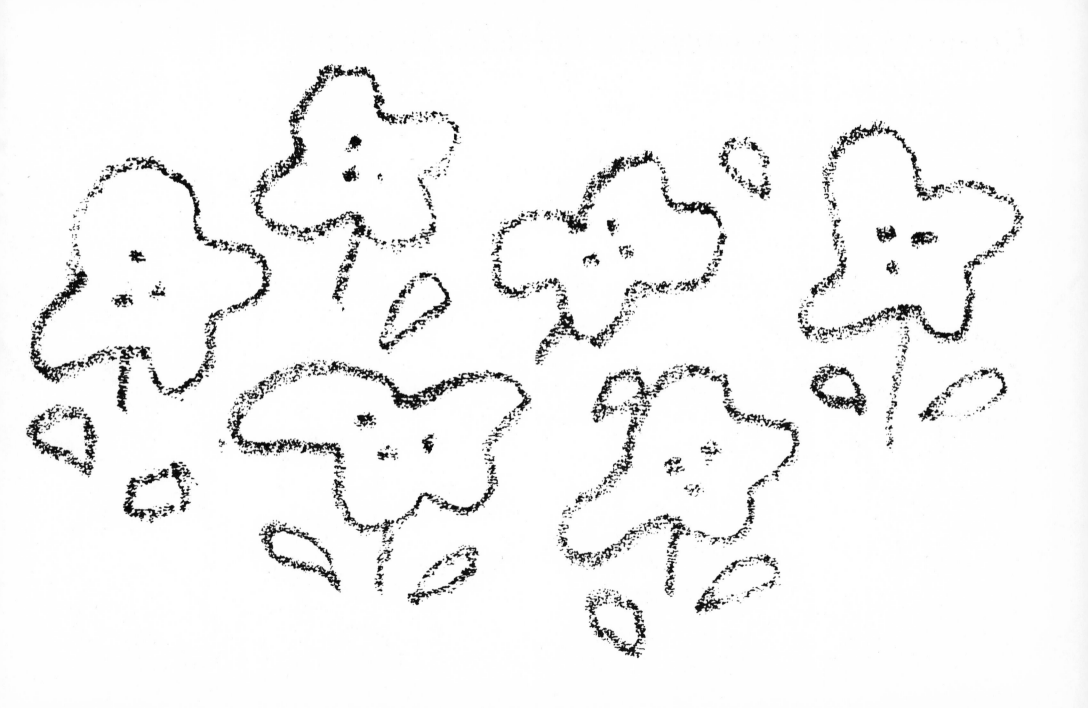

Draw 5 worms wriggling in the grass.
Now draw 5 beetles.

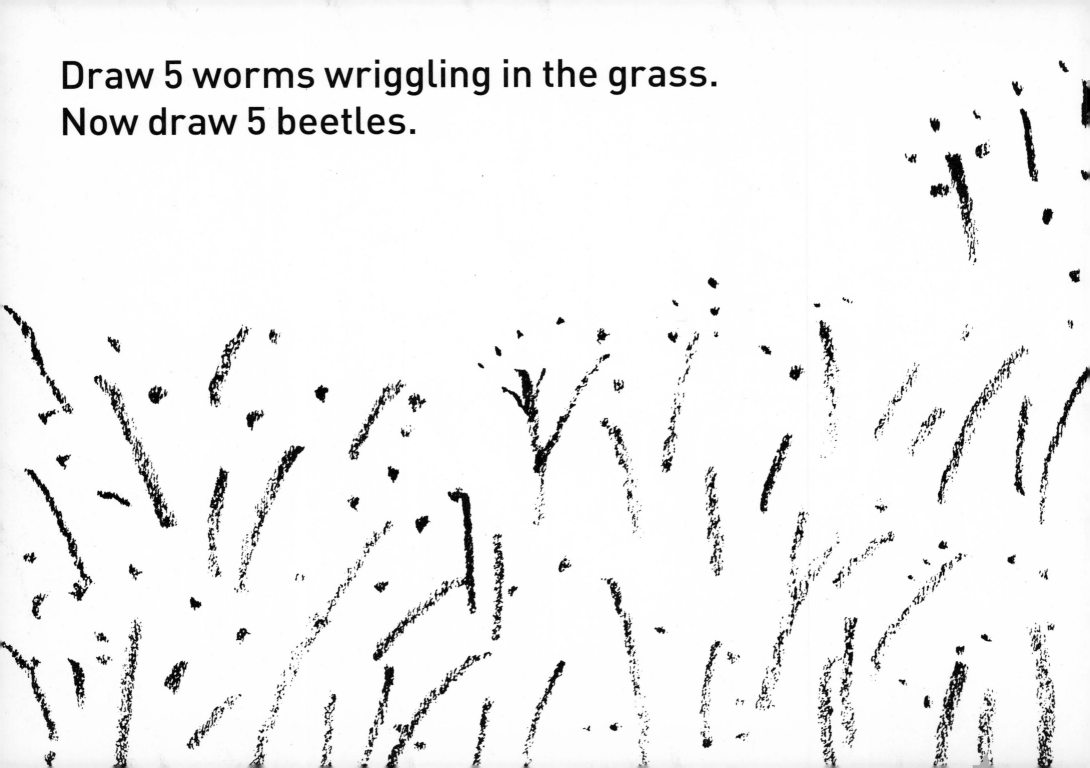

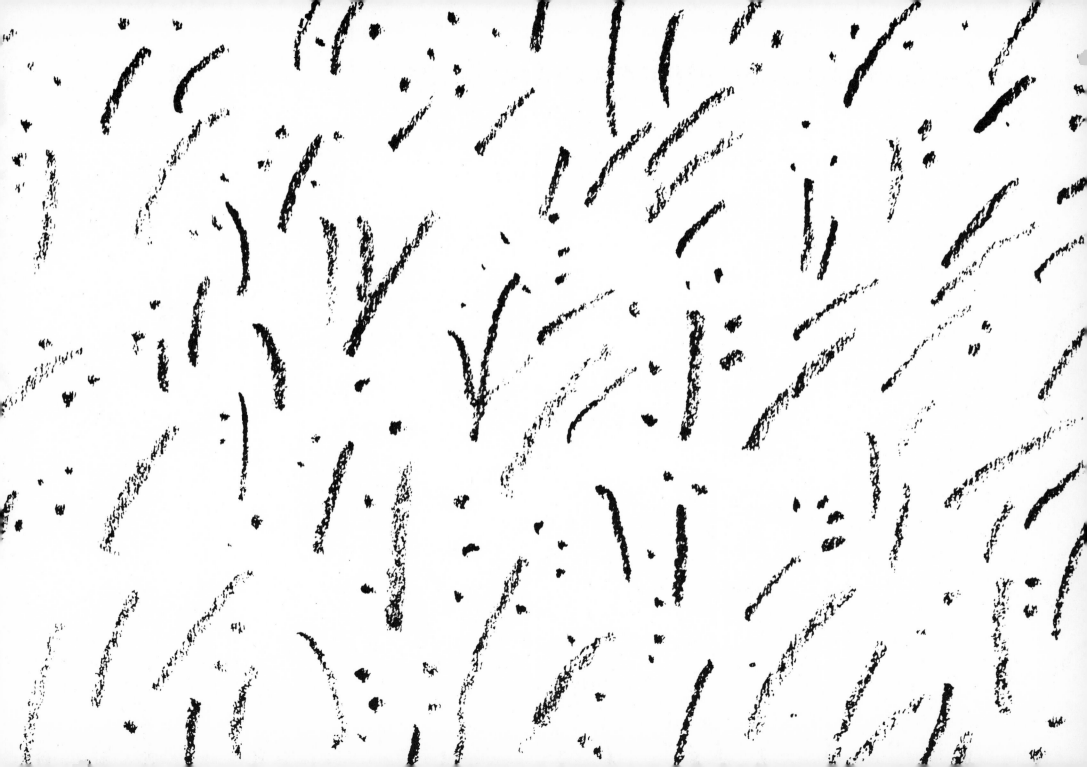

Draw 20 more mushrooms growing in the field.

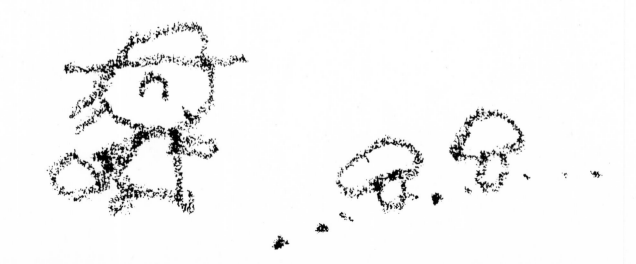

Draw 30 more cacti growing in the desert.

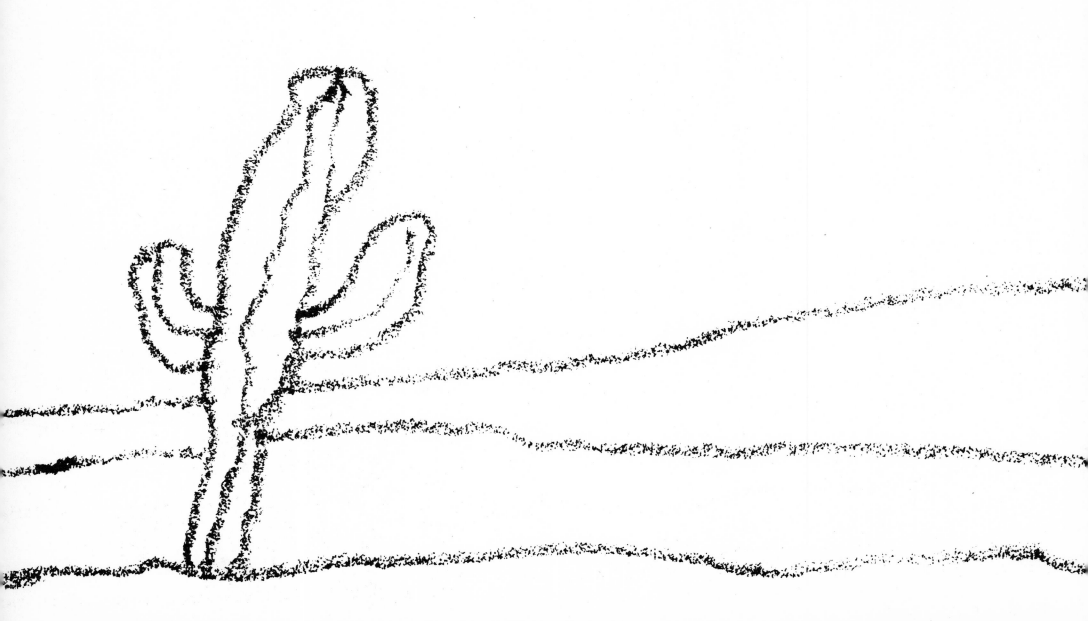

Draw 50 green leaves on the tree.

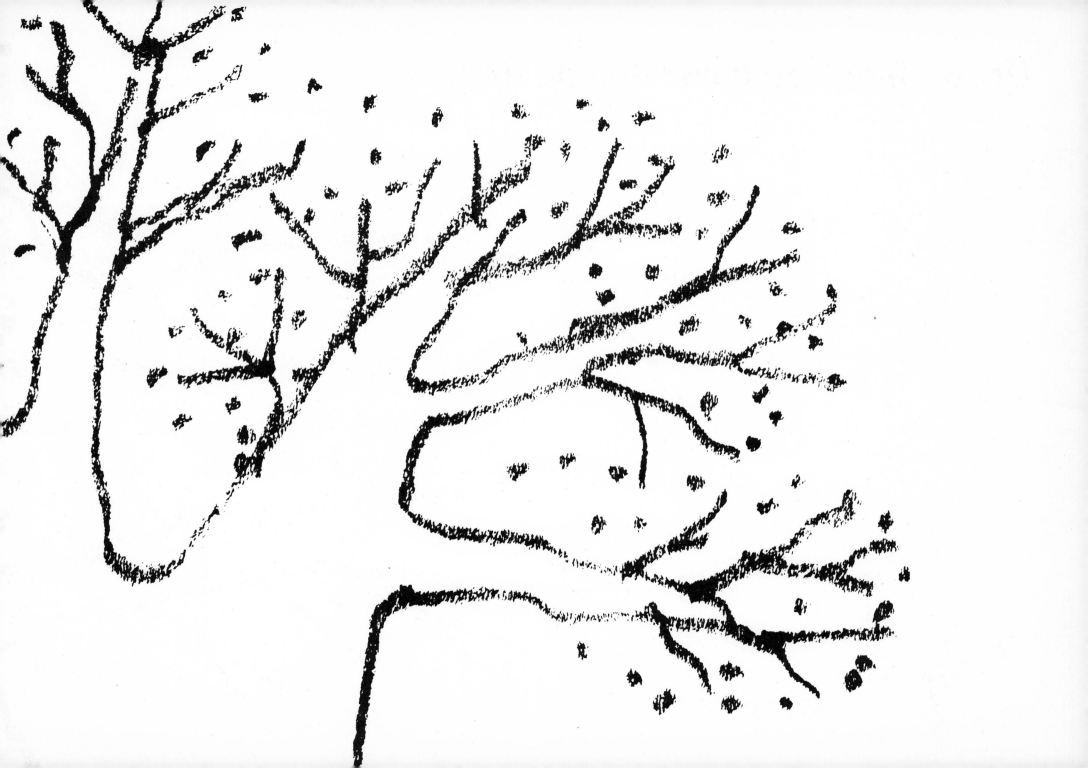

Draw 100 more trees on the hillside.

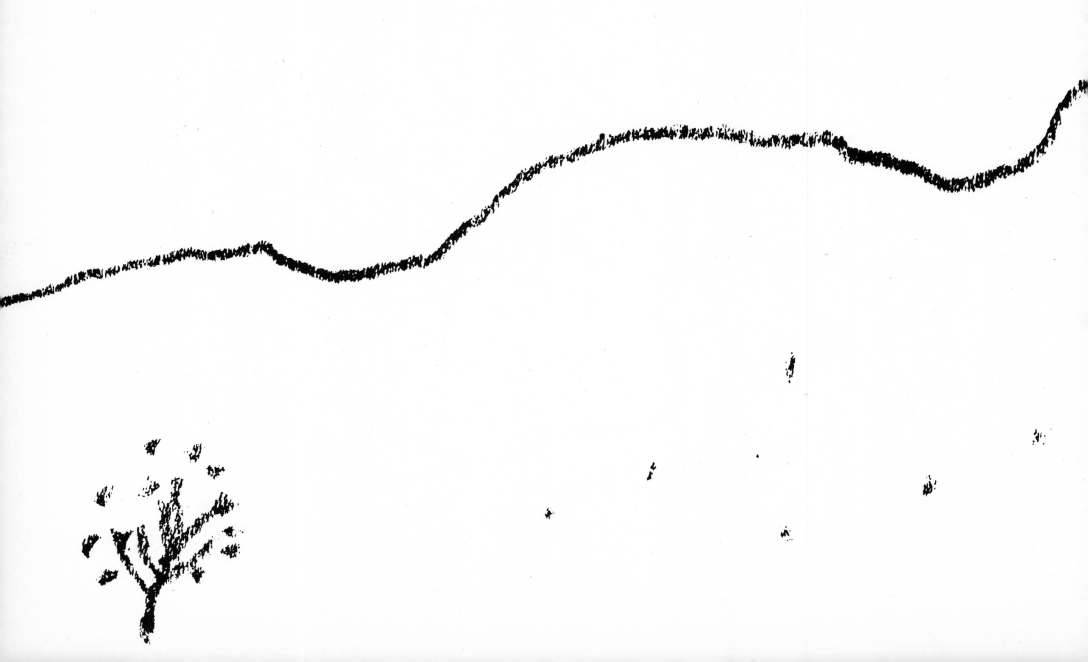

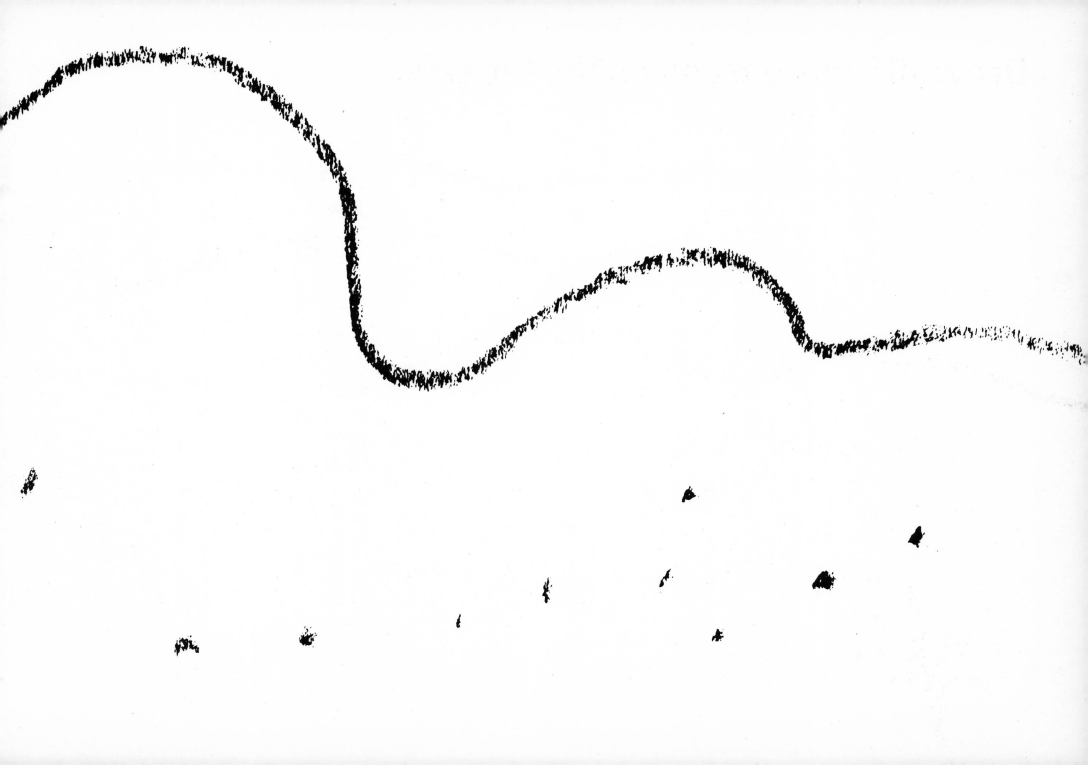

Draw 200 fish swimming in the sea.

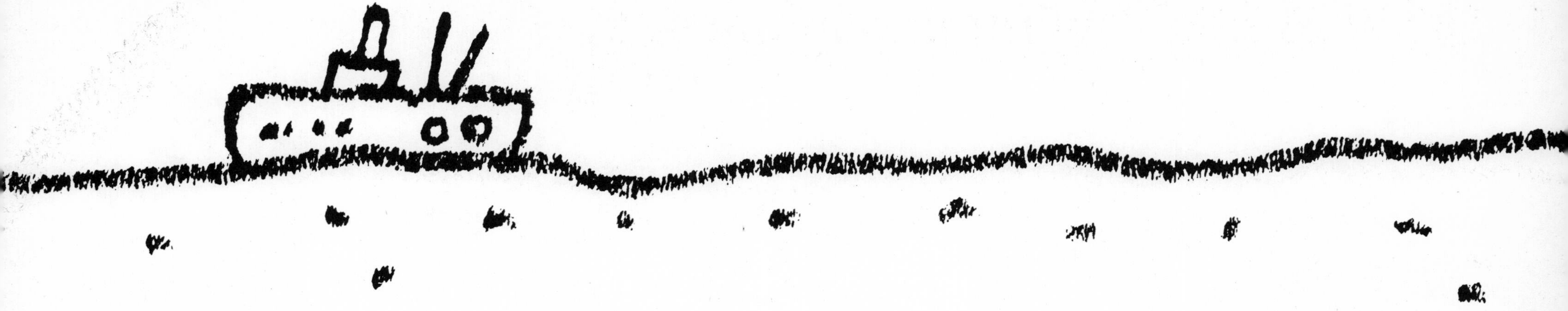

Draw 300 stars in the night sky.

Ask everyone to help you!

Colour these beetles but leave 13 plain.

Cut the bread into 5 slices.

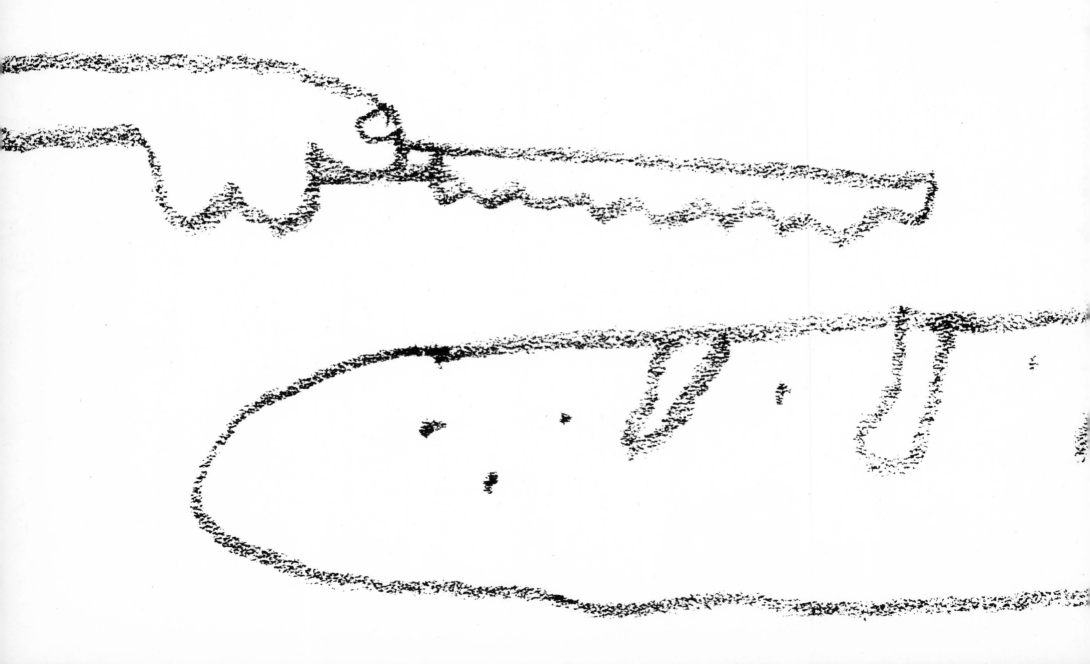

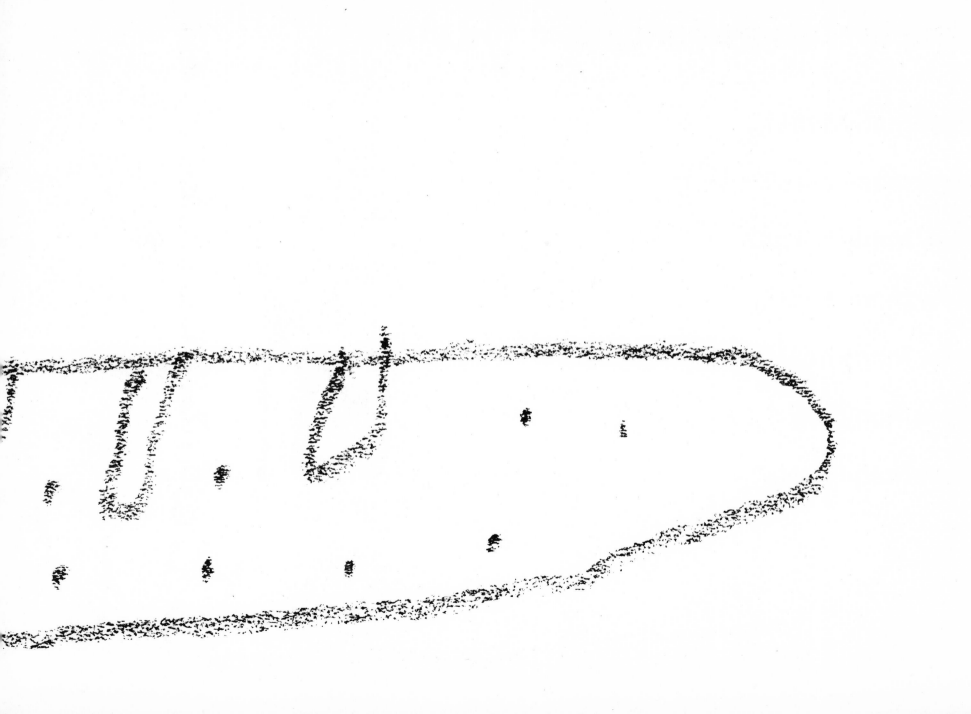

Look at this animal and fill in the blanks.

How many eyes?

How many ears?

How many horns?

How many tails?

How many noses?

How many legs?

How many spots?

Look at this monster and fill in the blanks.

How many eyes?

How many ears?

How many horns?

How many tails?

How many wings?

How many fangs?

How many teeth?

How many legs?

How many claws?

How many spots?

This face is made of numbers.
Make one of your own!

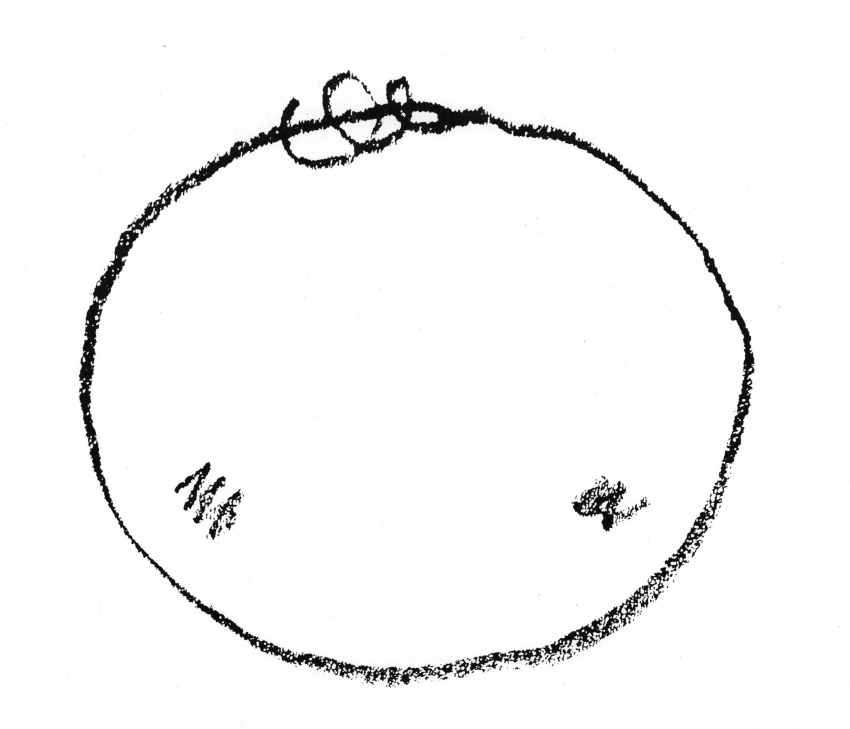

Use numbers to make pretty patterns on the bag and the dress.

Which man is bigger?
Which number is bigger?

Write a larger number in the empty spaces.

Write a smaller number in the empty spaces.

Help the teacher by marking this test!
Put a tick for the right answers and a cross for the wrong ones.

$1 + 2 = 3$

$3 + 4 = 8$

$5 + 9 = 14$

$6 + 10 = 19$

$8 + 7 = 13$

$5 - 3 = 2$

$10 - 6 = 6$

$2 - 1 = 1$

$3 \times 4 = 25$

$8 \div 2 = 4$

Marks out of 10:

What time is it?

_____ o'clock

What time is it now?

_____ o'clock

What time is it?

_____

And how about now?

_____

A triangle has 3 sides.
Draw your own triangle.

A square has 4 sides.
Draw your own square.

A pentagon has 5 sides.
Draw your own pentagon.

A hexagon has 6 sides.
Draw your own hexagon.

What costs the most?
What costs the least?

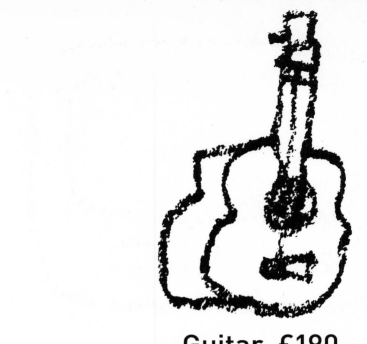

Guitar £190

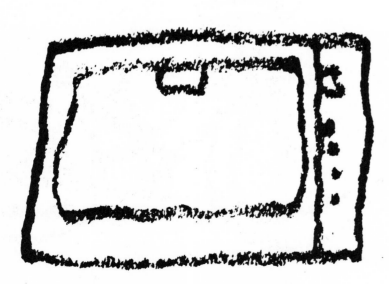

Microwave £165

Remote control car £30

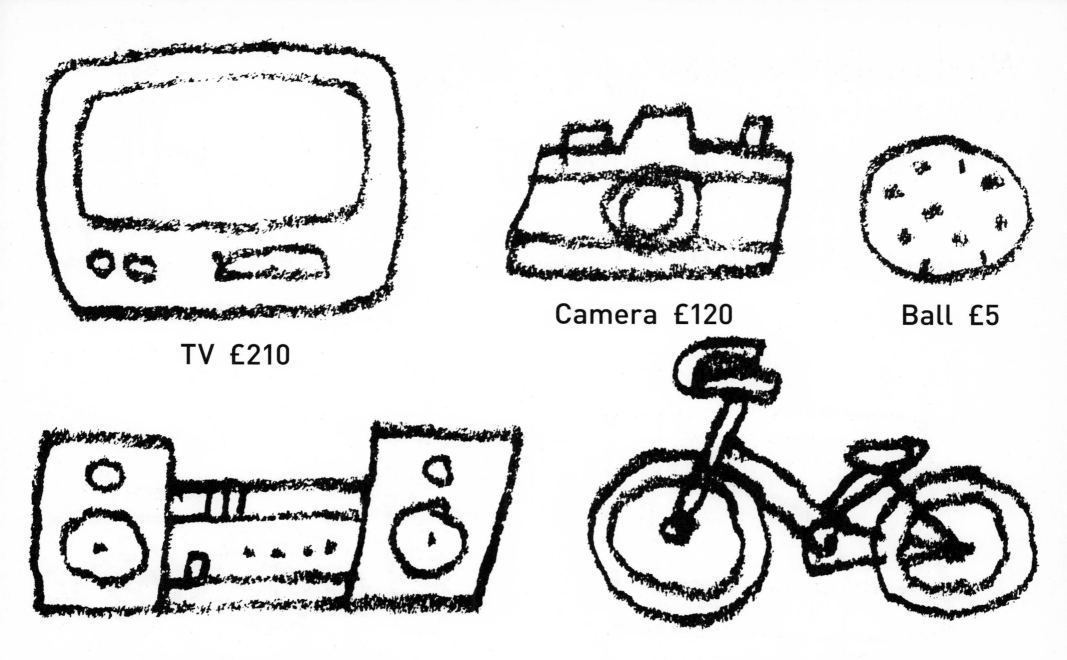

TV £210

Camera £120

Ball £5

Music system £320

Bike £140

Which tasty treat costs the most?

What can you buy for 50p?
What can you buy for £1?
What can you buy for £1.50?

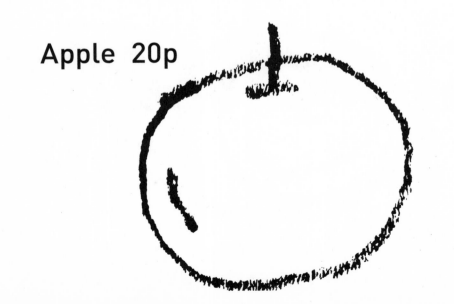

Apple 20p

Chocolate 40p

Sweet 5p

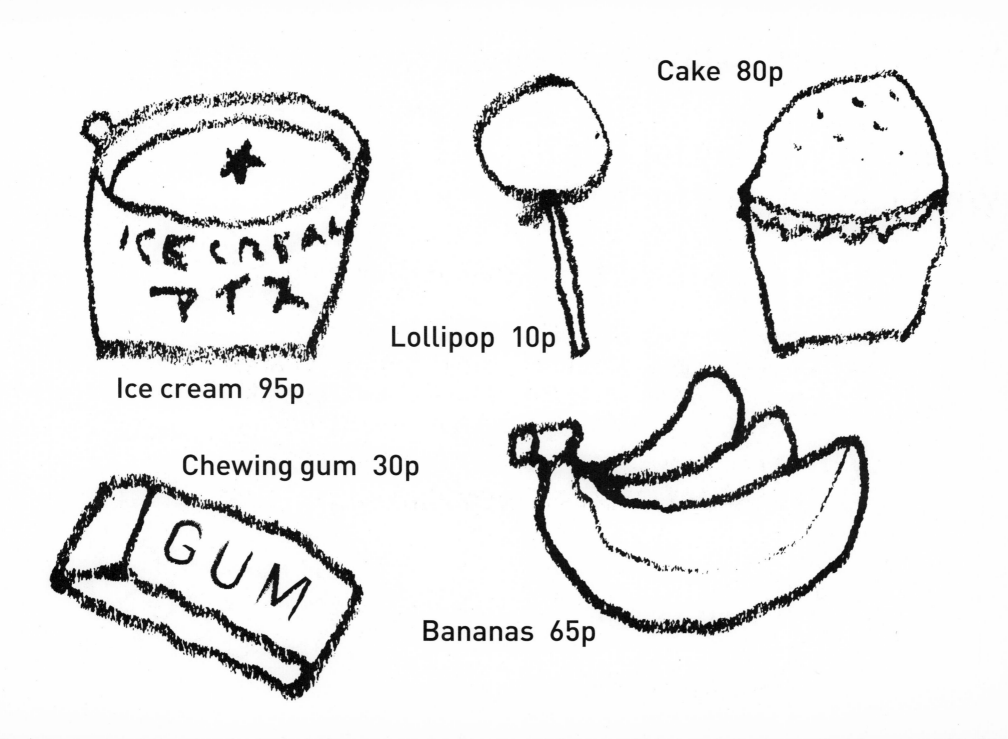

Cake 80p

Lollipop 10p

Ice cream 95p

Chewing gum 30p

Bananas 65p

Write the prices on the signs.

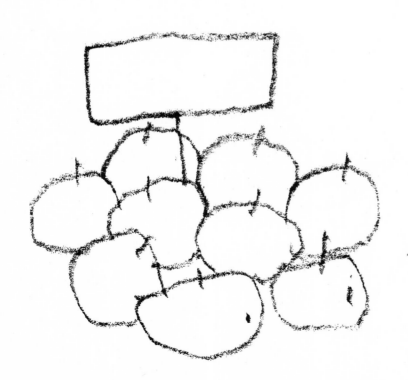

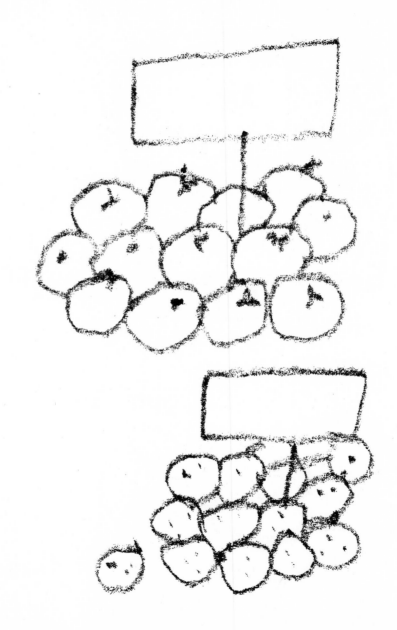

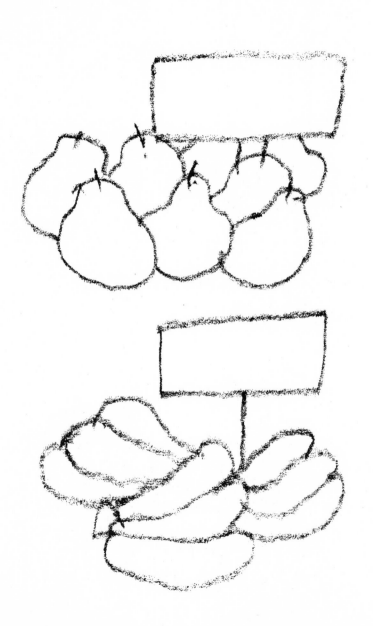

Write the price for each car.

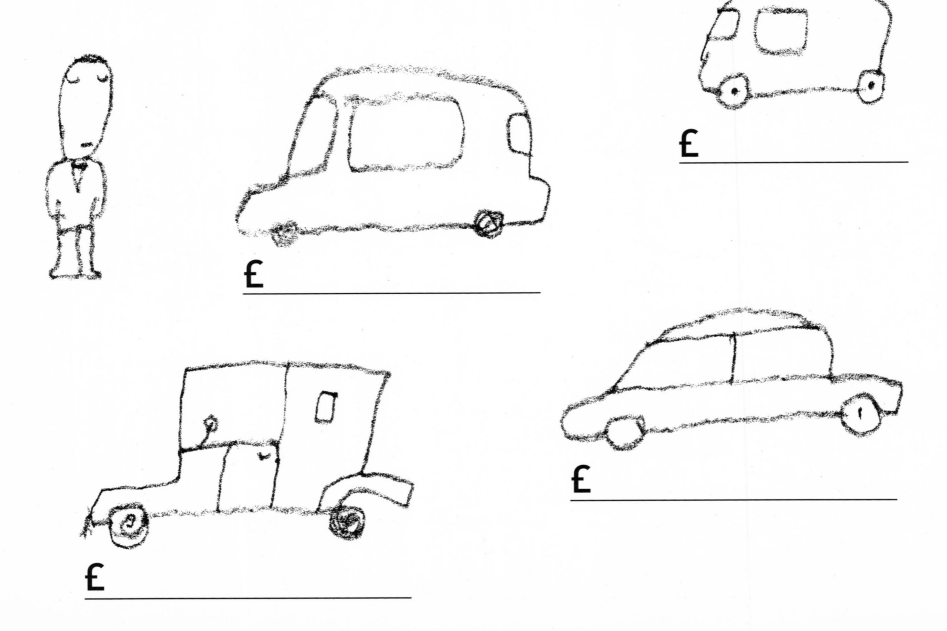

£ _____

£ _____

£ _____

£ _____

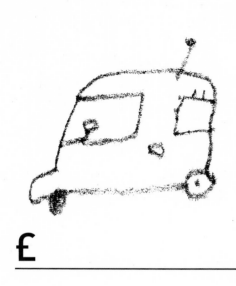

£ _____

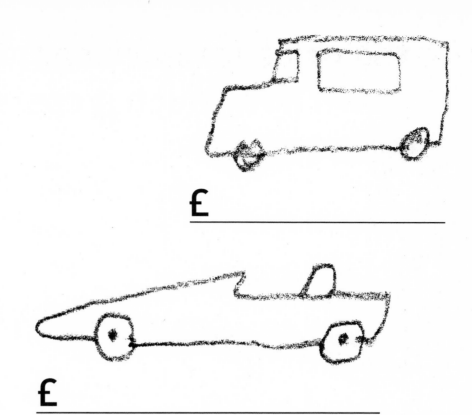

£ _____

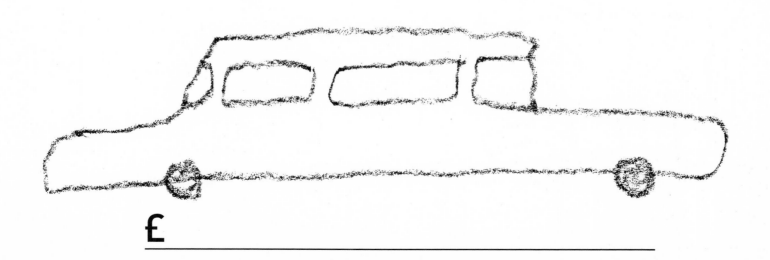

£ _____

£ _____

Use this credit card to buy yourself something nice!
Write down how much it costs underneath.

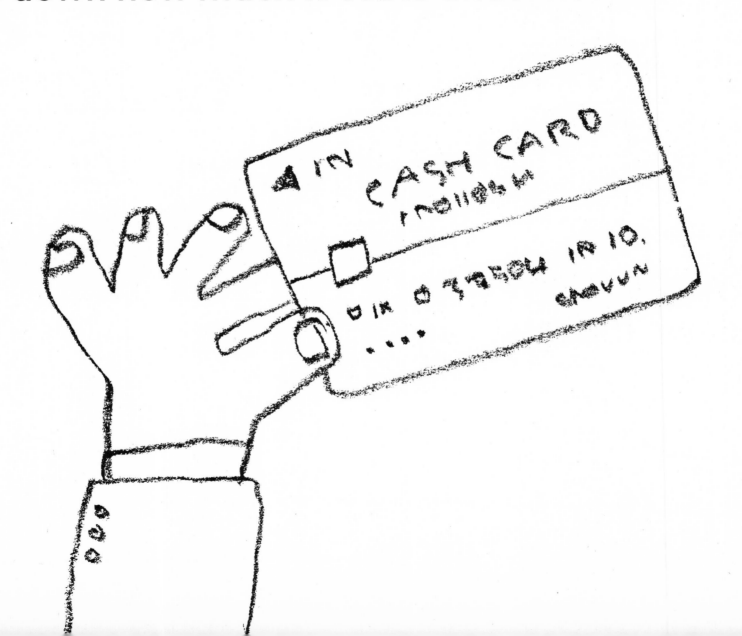

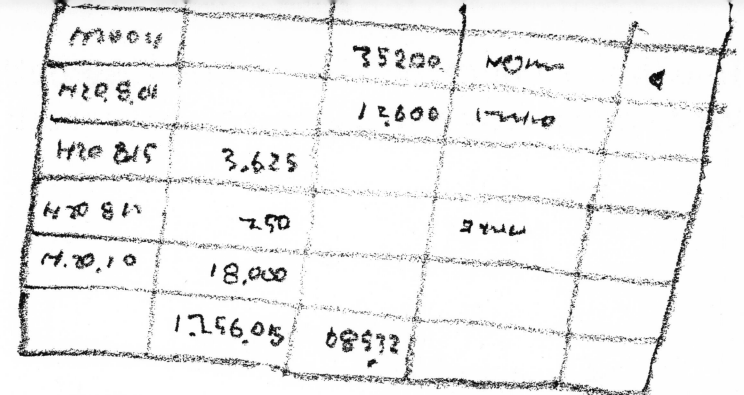

**Add up all your pocket money
and write down the total here.**

£ _____

How old do you think these people are?
Write their ages next to them.

Which monster is the scariest? Give them marks out of ten for scariness!

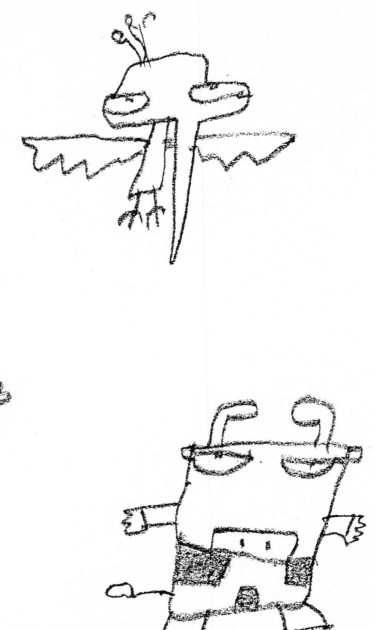

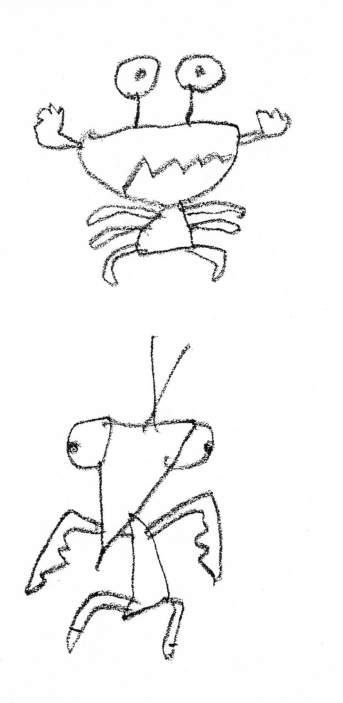
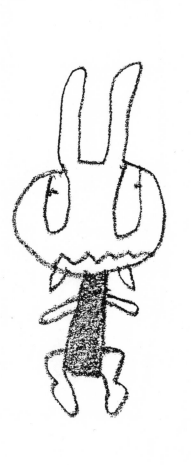

Which team has won – the Tigers or the Bears?
Add up their points.

T	1	2	3
T	O	O	O
B	1	O	2

4	5	6	7	8	9
3	0	1	1	2	0
1	0	0	0	0	2

Fill this pot up to the 2 litre mark.

Fill this one up to 2 and half litres.

It's 25° C today.
Colour the thermometer.

Colour this one to 5° C.
Brrr, it's rather cold!

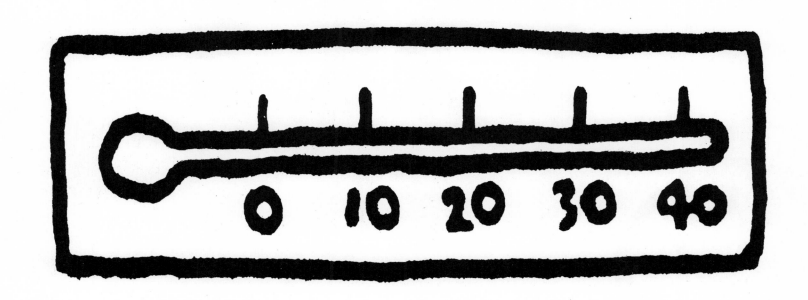

Write these numbers in words.

86

950

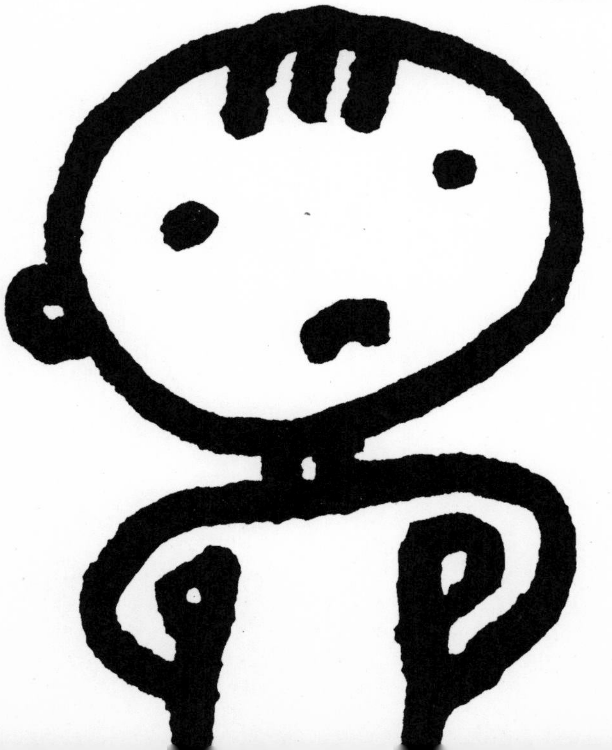

1057

26653049

Which crocodile has the biggest number?
What about when they're upside down?

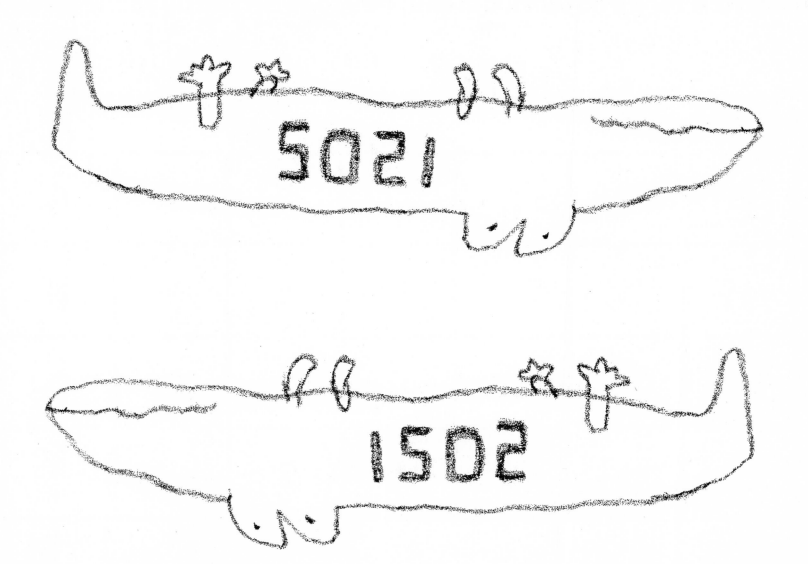

Here's a secret code!

Find the right letters and work out the message on the opposite page.

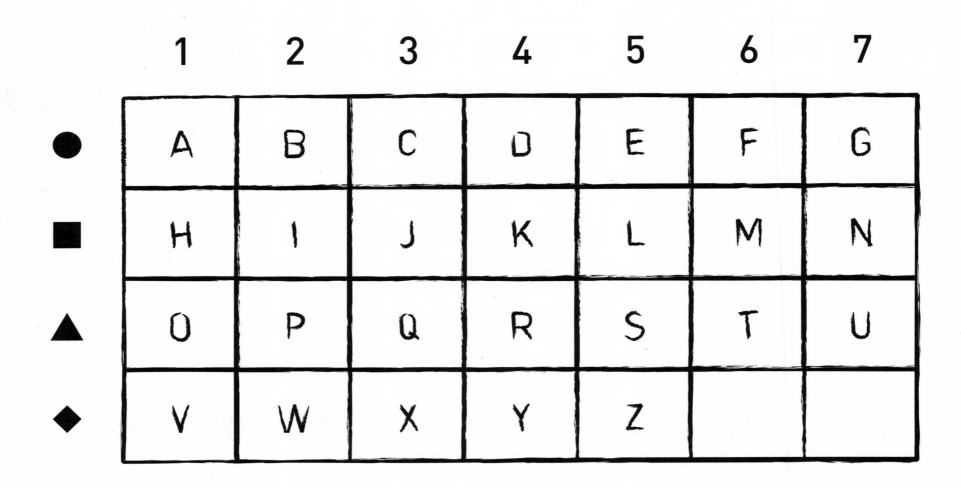

	1	2	3	4	5	6	7
●	A	B	C	D	E	F	G
■	H	I	J	K	L	M	N
▲	O	P	Q	R	S	T	U
◆	V	W	X	Y	Z		

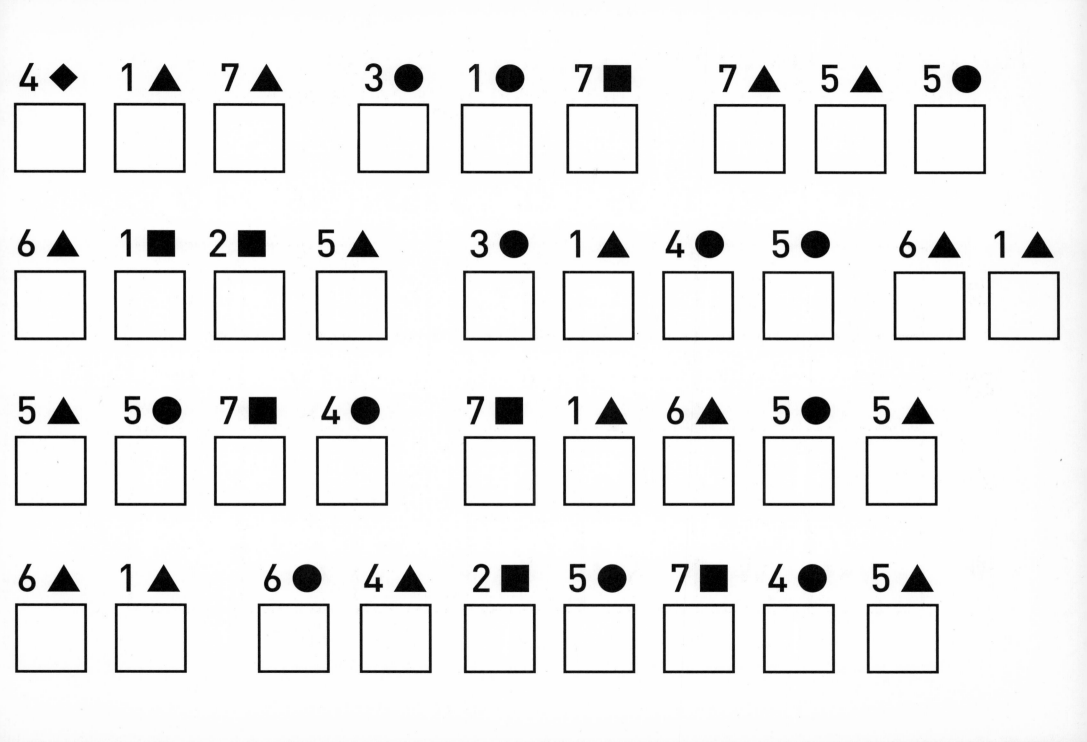

Find all the numbers and draw circles around them.

1	B	Y	5	O	⊃	3	L	M
9	X	2	∵	4	#	⊔	8	5
⊥	7	÷	11	K	↑	9	X	0
b	⊙	8	+	⋇	6	41	Y	~
⚲	15	↑	10	2	N	12	Z	3
22	P	R	13	→	0	9	8	?
3	1	51	b	6	b	T	21	V

∧	17	=	5	0	9	2	÷	7
4	>	π	O	12	*	4	8	×
C	5	22	∨	6	Z	C	⋯	9
H	11	8	~	2	3	w	6	L
9	→	C	P	6	7	0	∅	T
D	A	99	×	C	⌂	M	5	1
S	31	Z	C	4	U	R	2	19

Draw a line through the squares, counting from 1 to 16.
You can't move diagonally.

8	11	14	13
9	10	13	14
12	11	12	15	16

Now draw a line from 1 to 70 in the same way.

1	2	3	5	6	14	15	16	17	19
	3	4	7	12	13	16	15	18	20
	4	5	6	11	12	17	20	19	21
	8	6	9	10	13	19	21	20	22
	8	7	8	9	14	15	22	23	24
	9	10	12	13	15	17	20	24	25
	11	13	14	15	16	18	19	22	26

39	40	41	42	45	46	48	62	63	
38	41	44	43	44	45	46	61	62	
7	36	35	44	47	46	59	60	63	
4	25	34	45	48	49	58	65	64	
29	30	33	50	49	56	57	66	67	
28	31	32	51	54	55	56	68	68	
7	32	34	62	53	56	58	67	69	70

Follow the numbers and join the dots.

Can you guess what the picture will be?

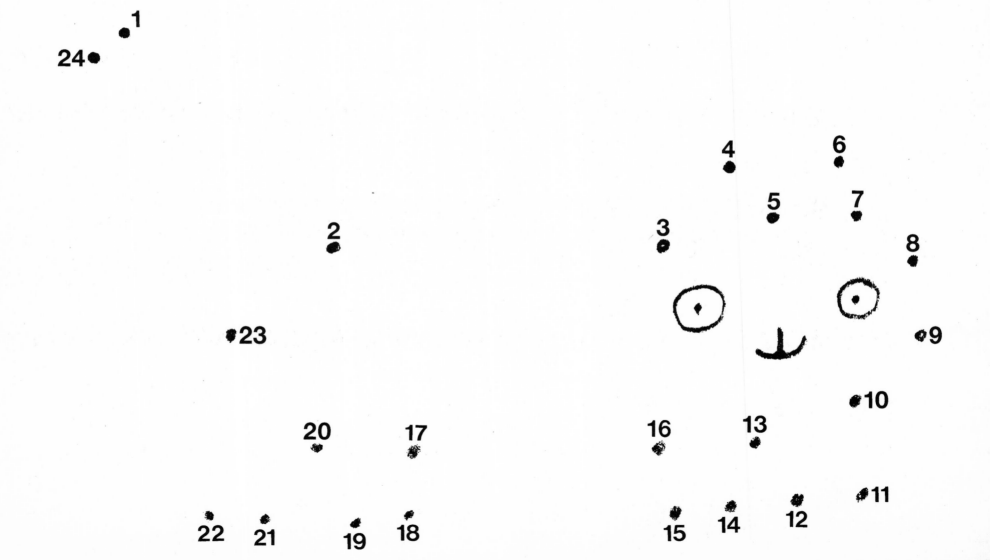

Now draw a line from 1 to 28.
Then draw another from (1) to (6).

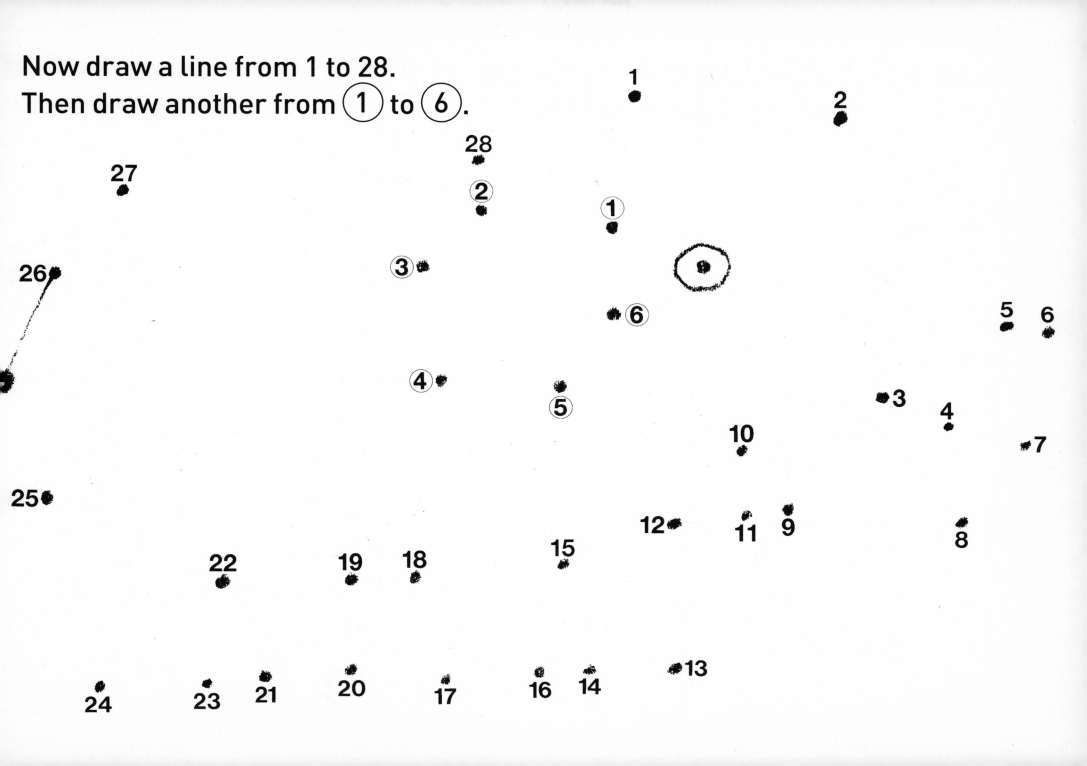

Now join these dots.
What do you think the picture will be?

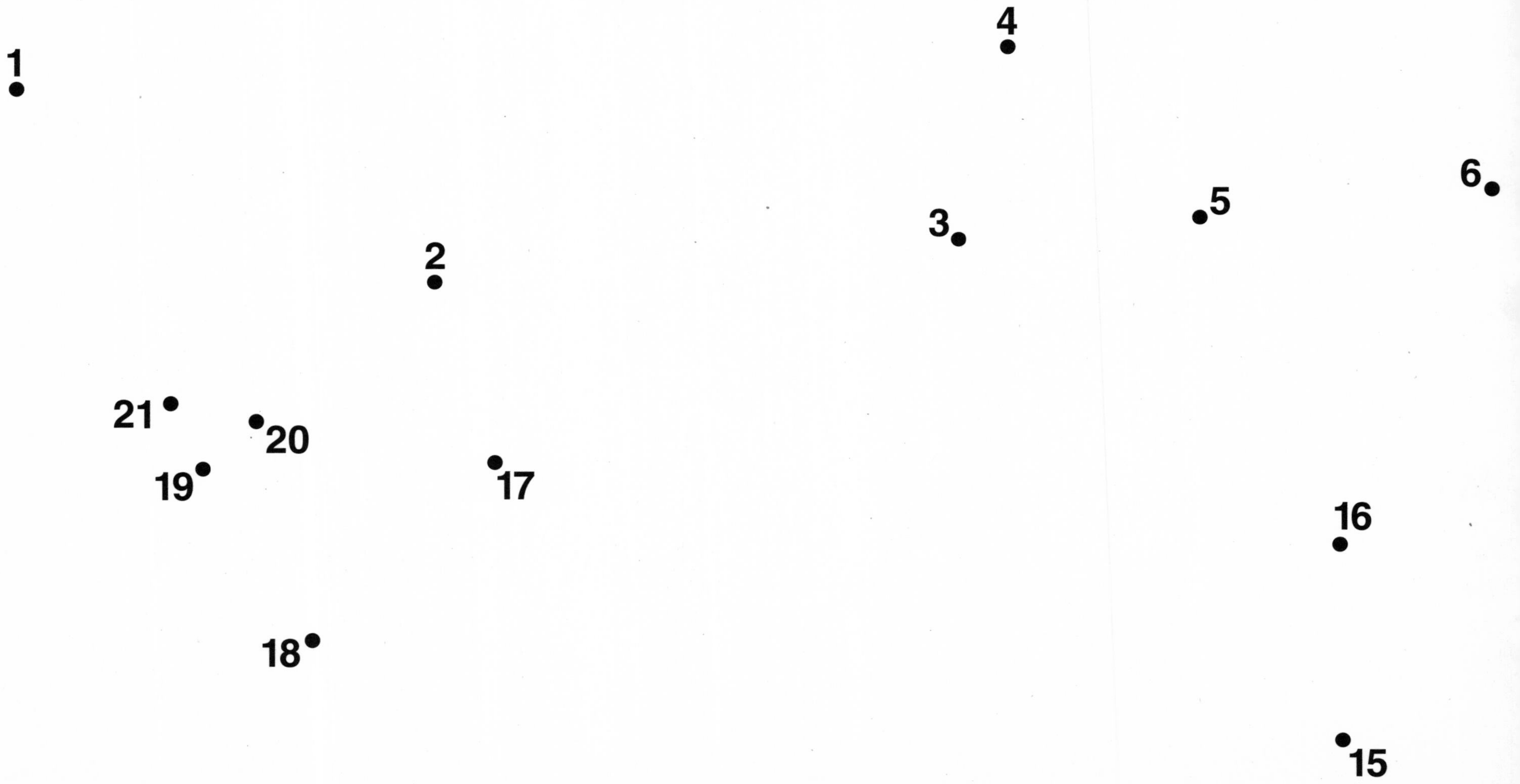

7

1

4

6

3 5

2

21
20
19
17

16

18

15

8

9

12

10

14

13

11

Join the stars together to make numbers.

Count 3 boxes down and 4 boxes to the right.
Colour this box black.

Count 3 boxes down
and 2 to the right.
Colour this box red.

Count 6 boxes down
and 5 from the left.
Colour this box
yellow.

Count 7 boxes
up and 8 to the
right. Colour this
box green.

Count 4 boxes
up and 2 from
the left. Colour
this box blue.

Colour by numbers!
Use the list below to help you.

1 – Red
2 – Green
3 – Yellow
4 – Blue
5 – Brown
6 – Purple
7 – Pink
8 – Orange
9 – Sky blue
10 – Grey
11 – Any colour you like!

Use the colour list for these pages too.

First published in the United Kingdom in 2010 by
Thames & Hudson Ltd, 181A High Holborn, London WC1V 7QX

thamesandhudson.com

Original edition *Rakugaki Ehon 1 2 3* published in Japanese
by Bronze Publishing Inc.
Copyright © 2008 Taro Gomi
Published by arrangement with Bronze Publishing Inc., Tokyo

British Library Cataloguing-in-Publication Data
A catalogue record for this book is available from the British Library

ISBN 978-0-500-28859-7

Printed in Singapore